Egyptian Mythology

DON NARDO

LUCENT BOOKS
A part of Gale, Cengage Learning

GALE
CENGAGE Learning·

Detroit • New York • San Francisco • New Haven, Conn • Waterville, Maine • London

LIBRARY OF CONGRESS CATALOGING-IN-PUBLICATION DATA

Nardo, Don, 1947-
  Egyptian mythology / By Don Nardo.
     pages cm. -- (Mythology and culture worldwide)
  Includes bibliographical references and index.
  ISBN 978-1-4205-0745-4 (hardcover)
  1. Mythology, Egyptian--Juvenile literature. I. Title.
  BL2441.3.N36 2013
  299'.3113--dc23

                                                    2013001512

Lucent Books
27500 Drake Rd.
Farmington Hills, MI 48331

ISBN-13: 978-1-4205-0745-4
ISBN-10: 1-4205-0745-1

Printed in the United States of America
2 3 4 5 6 7 17 16 15 14 13

TABLE OF CONTENTS

Map of Ancient Egypt

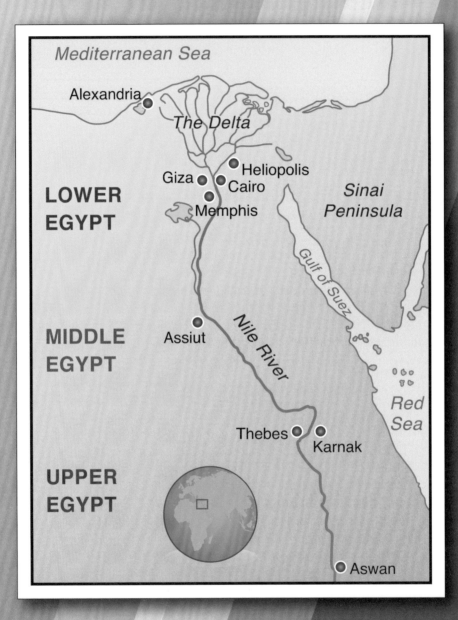

The Heliopolitan Theogony

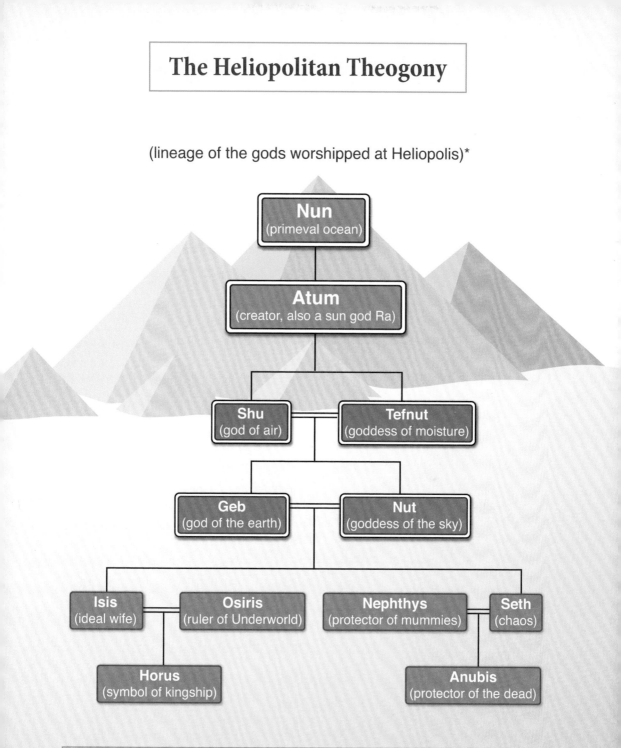

(lineage of the gods worshipped at Heliopolis)*

Nun
(primeval ocean)

Atum
(creator, also a sun god Ra)

Shu
(god of air)

Tefnut
(goddess of moisture)

Geb
(god of the earth)

Nut
(goddess of the sky)

Isis
(ideal wife)

Osiris
(ruler of Underworld)

Nephthys
(protector of mummies)

Seth
(chaos)

Horus
(symbol of kingship)

Anubis
(protector of the dead)

*The Heliopolitan cosmogony, or creation myth, in which these gods played roles, is the most famous of several creation stories from ancient Egypt. The nine gods beginning with Atum and ending with Seth were together seen as the sacred Ennead. The double lines indicate a marriage between two gods. It was common among Egyptian deities for brothers to marry their sisters.

Major Characters in Egyptian Mythology

Character Name	Pronunciation	Description
Amun	(AH-moon)	The creator god worshipped in the Egyptian city of Thebes. Amun became the sun god Amun Ra.
Atum	(AH-toom)	The creator god worshipped in the Egyptian city of Heliopolis.
Djehuty	(jeh-HOO-tee)	A military general under the pharaoh Tuthmosis III. Djehuty supposedly captured the Palestinian city of Joppa in an unusually clever manner.
Hathor	(HATH-er)	The cow-headed goddess of joy and love.
Horus	(HOR-us)	The divine son of Isis and Osiris. Horus fought Seth in the Myth of Kingship to obtain revenge for Osiris's murder.
Imhotep	(im-HOH-tep)	The architect who designed and erected Egypt's first pyramid and centuries later was recognized as a god.
Isis	(EYE-sis)	Egypt's widely popular mother-goddess who was known for her potent magical abilities, with which she brought her murdered husband, Osiris, back to life.
Khnum	(k'NOOM)	The ram-headed deity who fashioned the human race from clay.
Khonsu	(KON-su)	God of the moon. In one of his myths, the pharaoh Ramesses II asks him to drive a demon from a princess's body.
Osiris	(oh-SY-rus)	God of fertility and ruler of the Underworld, as well as Isis's husband. It was thought that deceased pharaohs became one with Osiris.
Ptah	(TAH)	The creator god worshipped in the Egyptian city of Memphis.
Ra (or Re)	(RAH)	The sun god, who journeyed across the sky in the daytime and fought monsters beneath the earth at night.

Ramesses	(RAM-uh-zeez, or RAM-zeez)	The name of eleven pharaohs of the New Kingdom; the greatest among them was Ramesses II, who had roles in some myths in the centuries following his reign.
Seth	(SETH)	Brother of Isis and Osiris, and a storm god. He killed Osiris out of jealousy and seized Eygpt's throne.
Sinuhe	(SIN-oo-ay)	A soldier under the pharaoh Senusret I. In his famous myth, Sinuhe went into self-exile but returned to Egypt in old age.
Thoth	(TOTE)	God of scribes, wisdom, and architecture and a minor player in numerous Egyptian myths.

Myths That Left the World Richer

I n the first few days of September 2012, a large crowd of angry people gathered outside the U.S. embassy in Cairo, the capital of modern Egypt. Some male members of the mob climbed over one of the walls surrounding the embassy compound and pulled down the American flag that normally flies there. They carried the flag back to the crowd. Then, as some of the protesters tore it apart, others chanted, "Say it, don't fear. Their ambassador must leave." A few minutes later, a group of women, clad in black robes, emerged from the throng. Their faces were obscured by veils, also black, so that only their eyes were visible. Waving their hands, they recited the words, "Worshippers of the Cross, leave the Prophet Muhammad alone"[1] several times in succession.

When reports of these happenings began to filter out to Western nations, including the United States, the protesters' motivations were at first uncertain. Then it became clear that they were upset over a short American-made movie that had recently appeared on YouTube. A fourteen-minute-long trailer (preview) of a full-length film, it portrays supposed incidents from the life of Muhammad, the prophet and founder of the Islamic faith. In the trailer, he is depicted as a fake religious leader who is interested only in having sex and killing people.

It did not take long for the protests over the movie trailer to spread from Egypt to other Muslim countries. In the meantime, the nature of the offending film was increasingly revealed. It turned out that the man who made it was thought to be Nakoula Basseley, an Egyptian Christian with a history of anti-Muslim activities. Furthermore, evidence showed that no full-length version of the film existed. Rather, Basselely had produced only the trailer and put it on the Internet hoping to stir up trouble.

The World's Most Religious People?

In the wake of these incidents, some Western commentators pointed out that it was neither a coincidence nor a surprise that Middle Eastern protests against the trailer had originated in Egypt. After all, they said, the filmmaker had attacked the religious beliefs held by Egyptians and most of their neighbors in the region. Today, those beliefs happen to be based in Islam. With more than a billion followers across the globe, Islam is one of the world's three great monotheistic faiths. (The other two are Christianity and Judaism.)

Yet it was not only Islam that the protesters were defending. On a deeper level it was religious faith itself. Throughout their history, no matter what the nature of their beliefs, the Egyptians have been staunchly and devoutly religious. Indeed, when the Greek historian Herodotus visited Egypt in the fifth century B.C., more than a millennium before Islam arose, the depth of that religious devotion astounded him. The Egyptians "are religious to excess, beyond any other nation in the world,"[2] he declared.

Herodotus noted that, like the Greeks, the Egyptians of that era were polytheistic; that is, they believed in and worshipped multiple gods. Moreover, he learned the stories of the Egyptian gods—the myths that explained how those deities had come into being, how they had created the human race, and how they continued to receive sacrifices and other worship from humans.

Herodotus was highly observant. He recognized certain strong similarities between the Egyptian gods, myths, and rituals and those of his native land. He also realized that Egyptian society was far older than that of Greece. Indeed,

Modern-day Egyptians demonstrate in support of Islam outside a mosque in Cairo. Throughout Egypt's history, no matter what religion they have practiced, Egyptians have been devout.

Herodotus suspected that the Egyptians might be "the most ancient" of "all races in the world." He came to believe that they were the first people on earth to recognize the gods, as well as "the first to assign altars and images and temples to the gods, and to carve figures in stone." In fact, he said, Egypt was at first "ruled by the gods, who lived on earth amongst men."[3] The last divine being to sit on Egypt's throne was Horus, Herodotus wrote, after whose reign Egypt was ruled by human kings for more than eleven thousand years. That made the Egyptian lands lying along the banks of the mighty Nile River a true cradle of human civilization.

From his belief in the great age of the Egyptian nation, Herodotus made the logical leap that at least some of Egypt's gods and myths had influenced the religions of later peoples, including the Greeks. The identities, or roles, of the gods, he wrote in his now famous history book, *The Histories*, "were brought into Greece from Egypt." The Pelasgians, the inhabitants of Greece before the first Greek speakers arrived, absorbed these identities, he suggested. "From that time onward, therefore, the Pelasgians used the [identities] of the gods in their sacrifices, and from the Pelasgians"[4] these gods passed on to later Greek society— the culture into which Herodotus was born.

Oracles of Amun and Zeus

Some of the proof Herodotus offered to support this theory consisted of certain similarities between Egypt's leading god and that deity's Greek counterpart, Zeus. In the major Egyptian city of Thebes, the god was called Amun, or Amun-Ra (also seen as Amun-Re). Herodotus referred to him as the "Theban Zeus." In Greece, especially at Dodona, in the north, the god was called Zeus Ammon.

One of these similarities that Herodotus pointed to was the fact that Amun-Ra in Egypt and Zeus Ammon in Greece both had widely popular oracles. In ancient times an oracle was a priest or priestess who, it was thought, could relay the words or will of a god to humans. "It is certainly true," Herodotus said, "that the oracles at Thebes and Dodona are similar in character."[5] Moreover, he wrote, a third famous oracle of the same god existed in Libya, which lay directly west of Egypt.

The Egyptians themselves were well aware of the parallels among their worship of Amun-Ra, the Greeks' worship of Zeus Ammon, and worship of that same deity in Libya. In fact, they had an ancient myth that purported to explain how these similarities came about, and they told it to Herodotus. "According to the priests of the Theban Zeus," he stated in his book, "two women connected with the service of [Amun's] temple [in Thebes] were carried off by the Phoenicians [traders who lived along the coast of Palestine] and sold, one in Libya and the other in Greece. And it was these women who founded the oracles in the two [other] countries."[6] Thus, people today know about that myth, along with some other ancient Egyptian myths and religious customs,

The Egyptian god Amun-Ra appears in a bas-relief of the temple of Beit al Wali. The ways in which Amun-Ra was worshipped are very similar to the ways the ancient Greek deity Zeus Ammon was worshipped.

because Herodotus took the time to describe them in writing. Otherwise, they may well have been lost over the course of the ensuing centuries. Furthermore, he was not the only ancient foreigner who commented on Egyptian religious beliefs and myths and in the process passed some of them on to later ages. The second-century A.D. Roman writer Lucius Apuleius was one of several others. In his charming novel *The Golden Ass,* he recorded a number of stories and rituals associated with Egyptian divinities.

In particular, Apuleius described Isis, a renowned Egyptian mother goddess whom the Greeks and Romans of his day had come to worship as well. In the most famous of her many myths, she tracked down the scattered body parts of her murdered and dismembered brother, Osiris. She then reassembled the parts and, using her potent magic, brought him back to life.

Apuleius revered and respected Isis and her rituals and myths. In contrast, another second-century A.D. Roman writer, Juvenal (born Decimus Junius Juvenalis), was far less kind in his writings about the Egyptian gods. "Who has not heard," he asked in one of his popular social satires (literary spoofs), "of the monstrous deities those crazy Egyptians worship?" He proceeded to ridicule how many Egyptian gods took the form of animals in art, worship, and myths, as opposed to the Greco-Roman deities, who were nearly always depicted in human form. One group of Egyptians, he said,

> adores crocodiles, another worships the snake-gorged ibis [a large wading bird]. And where . . . old [Egyptian] Thebes, with her hundred gates, now lies in ruins, there gleams the golden effigy [statue] of a long-tailed monkey. You'll find whole cities devoted to cats, or to river-fish, or dogs—but not a soul who worships Diana [the Roman goddess of hunting, for whom the dog was a symbol].[7]

Relics of a Bygone Culture

Although Juvenal poked fun at several Egyptian gods and their myths, in the process he recorded in writing some of the events from those ancient stories. So he, too, helped to perpetuate them. Meanwhile, the average Egyptian was a peasant-farmer who worked from dawn to dusk to scratch out a meager living. Unable to read and write, he or she had never heard of Juvenal nor any other glib poet writing for educated, upscale city folk in faraway places like Rome.

Nor did the vast majority of Egyptians, whether poor or rich, care what foreigners thought of their gods and myths. The people of Egypt *knew* those deities were real and that those stories were true. This was because, as Herodotus had pointed out, religiously speaking the Egyptians were extraordinarily devout. They were certain in their hearts that the fulsome heritage of rich, colorful, inspiring, and entertaining myths handed down to them by their ancestors explained how the world and human civilization had come to be. So they dutifully passed on the tales of the gods from one generation to the next.

What is more, even after the ancient religion that spawned those myths disappeared, these stories lived on. Later peoples—Christians, Jews, Muslims, and others alike—saw them as quaint, imaginative relics of a bygone culture. But not just any culture. It turned out that Herodotus had been right in his assumption that the ancient Egyptians had created one of the so-called cradles of human civilization. That noteworthy distinction alone made their singular body of myths appear fascinating and worth preserving. As former British Museum scholar George Hart explains it,

> Egyptian myths, though seemingly outlandish to some, have survived because the society out of which they originated considered them crucial to the creation of a view of the world. Scribes, priests, and storytellers transmitted myths to explain [the wonders of nature], to provide data for the continuity of existence in the afterlife, and to exhibit the versatility of their imaginations. So, whether as part of a religious quest or . . . for an adventure into the surreal [bizarre or dreamlike], the myths and legends of ancient Egypt leave us richer for their speculation and imagery.[8]

CHAPTER 1

Origins of Egyptian Gods and Myths

In exotic Egypt, countless centuries ago when the gods still sometimes walked among humans, Isis arrived at a small town near the Nile River's delta. A deity known for her potent magical abilities, she was protected by several gigantic scorpions that did her bidding. Isis first went to the door of a rich woman's house and asked if she could stay the night. But the mansion's mistress rudely told her to go away and slammed the door shut. The scorpions were angered at this rebuff. So when the goddess proceeded to the next home, they sneaked into the rich woman's house and stung her small son almost to death. Isis soon found out what had happened. Taking pity on the boy, she used her magic to heal him, after which his mother had a change of heart. Thankful for what the goddess had done, she gave much of her fortune away to her poorer neighbors.

This myth, which was widely popular in ancient Egypt, did more than showcase Isis's miraculous powers. It also taught a moral lesson about the importance of hospitality. Today, more often than not, such mythical tales are viewed as quaint or charming stories about eras, peoples, and events of the past. In most cases, someone trots out one or more of these old stories to exploit their entertainment value, for instance, in a painting, graphic novel, or film. Or those myths are used to demonstrate the supposed simplicity or primitiveness of people in bygone ages. The notion that the events and themes of ancient myths are directly meaningful to present society and daily life is alien to modern thinking.

That notion was far from foreign to the ancient Egyptian worldview, however. To the Egyptians, their myths both explained how life and society came to be and provided helpful guidance in how to worship the gods, obey the pharaoh (king), and properly conduct oneself in everyday affairs. In historian George Hart's words, many of those myths

> formed an active, integral element in ancient Egyptian government and society. They were far from being a series of fossilized [accounts of] gods and goddesses. [Many] stand out as the projections of the ancient Egyptians' thoughts, hopes, and fears about the human condition and the troubles experienced in the course of one lifetime.[9]

A World Without Change

One important reason why average ancient Egyptians saw myths as having relevance to their own lives and society as a whole was that they did not see those stories as outdated, as people generally do today. Like most other ancient peoples, the Egyptians had little or no sense of history or progress. They did not imagine that life or the world would be significantly different in the future. So to them, their way of life had not developed over time from a less advanced form, nor would it develop into a *more* advanced form in the future. Rather, as noted scholar H.W.F. Saggs points out, ancient peoples viewed the existing world as

> something which the gods had decreed in the beginning and which had existed unchanged forever. With no concept of social progress, they had no incentive to make a conscious record of life in the thousand years before 2500 B.C., when some of the most momentous advances in human society were taking place.[10]

As a result, the Egyptians did not write formal histories to record the events of their world for the benefit of future societies. Instead, they maintained their heritage of myths, stories that told how divine forces and beings had shaped the heavens, earth, and human race. Once these things had been created, the residents of Egypt believed, they would continue in more or less the same form virtually forever. In this world without change, the major myths were like a set of blueprints that not only outlined the gods' and life's origins, but also ensured they would be eternally perpetuated. So it was essential to honor those stories and keep them safe inside the hearts and minds of Egyptians in each succeeding generation.

Early Egyptians maintained their mythic traditions through telling stories—often set to music—of how divine forces and beings shaped the heavens, earth, and human race.

Also in their minds was the assumption that, like Egypt's physical attributes, including the life-giving Nile River, religious worship had existed unchanged since the earliest days of their civilization. In this, they were more or less correct. Modern archaeologists have confirmed that ancient

Egyptian Time Periods

For convenience, modern historians divide ancient Egypt's long history into three major time periods (also seen as various stages of the Egyptian nation) called "kingdoms," as well as several shorter "intermediate" and other periods. The Old Kingdom, lasting from 2686 to 2181 B.C., is sometimes called the pyramid age because most of Egypt's pyramids, including all the large ones, were erected in that period. The Middle Kingdom spanned the years 2055 to 1650 B.C. In the century that followed—known as the Second Intermediate Period, a foreign people known as the Hyksos invaded Egypt and occupied most of its northern sector. During those years, the pharaohs ruled from Thebes, located far to the south. Ahmose, the first pharaoh of the New Kingdom, which spanned 1550 to 1069 B.C., drove the Hyksos out and launched Egypt's great age of empire, when it expanded northward into Palestine and Syria. The Late Period (747–332 B.C.) witnessed Egypt's occupation and rule by one foreign group after another.

Egyptian religion, in one form or another, was extremely old. As far back as the start of what these experts call the Predynastic Period (ca. 5500–3100 B.C.), certain now-familiar gods were already recognized and worshipped.

In that early period, these divine deities were associated with major natural objects, forces, and cycles that people could not understand or explain. No one knew, for example, what caused the Nile's annual floods. That mighty waterway flows for 4,130 miles (6,646km) northward, dividing the country roughly in half. Running alongside its ancient banks were a few miles of fertile land, forming a narrow green ribbon containing nearly all of the country's inhabitants. Beyond that verdant band stretched seemingly endless reaches of arid wasteland where almost no one dwelled. Even most of the areas along the riverbanks would have been unlivable if not for the fact that the Nile gently flooded over those banks each year. The water from these floods irrigated farmers' fields and thereby made it possible to grow the food necessary to maintain civilization.

Trying to Understand Nature

Equally mysterious to the earliest residents of the Nile Valley were the disappearance and reappearance of the sun each day, the true nature of the stars and other heavenly bodies, and other mysteries of nature. Because people could not explain these wonders, they came to view them as the works of beings far superior to humans—the gods. Recognizing, naming, and worshipping those divine beings gave people comfort. Believing that the gods controlled the natural world, humans felt that they could understand at least some key aspects of that world. Moreover, such understanding was a crucial step toward people themselves exerting some indirect control, however small, over nature. For instance, if they honored a god through prayer or sacrifice, that deity might do something beneficial for them; or at least the god might refrain from punishing them for their mistakes. Thus, recognizing and worshipping the gods, Egyptologist David Silverman explains, was the first step in trying

> to distinguish between the individual and the world in which that individual lived. Moreover, that step was taken to gain some control over the phenomena of nature. . . . At first [a god] would seem awesome and mysterious, but once it could be comprehended as a [conscious being], it could be recognized, understood, and then reinterpreted in a familiar and recurrent form. In a way, the force could be harnessed. It became humanized. That is, it was put in terms the individual could understand.[11]

One way to humanize the sun, for example, was to make its movements understandable. At some point, the earliest humans must have not only wondered at the nature of that glowing globe that crossed the sky in the daytime but also feared it might not return the next morning. Humanizing the sun by giving it a name and inventing a myth that explained why it *would* return each morning was a way to remove that primitive fear.

This was likely the origin of a familiar Egyptian myth about the sun god Ra (or Re). He crossed the sky in the daytime from east to west in his so-called Boat of Millions of Years. After he slipped beneath the horizon and darkness settled on Egypt, the story went, he encountered monsters on the far side of the known world. Of these, the most often cited in the myths was a frightening god of chaos called Apophis, who had the form of a giant serpent. Ra battled and defeated Apophis each night, ensuring that the sun's bright disk would return to herald the dawn of a new day.

Another way to put the gods in terms the individual could understand was to picture those beings in either human or animal form. These were, after all, the physical shapes that people viewed as most natural and comprehensible. Endowing a god with an animal's form was also a way to explain why certain nonhuman creatures were so vital to the ongoing existence and survival of human civilization.

One of the clearest examples was cattle. Cattle supplied meat, milk, hides, and other basic essentials, as well as pulled plows and wagons. Cattle became so important to the earliest Egyptians that people believed they were a gift from the gods. What better way to give such a gift, the thinking may have gone, than to wrap it in the very physical form of one or more gods. A number of scholars think that this is how the Egyptians concluded that the bovine form must be somehow connected to the divine. Here, then, may have been the origin of a very early goddess named Mehet-Weret, who had a cow's head. She was likely the precursor of the more important bovine goddess, Hathor, one of Ra's daughters.

Perhaps because cattle were so beneficial to humans, Hathor gained the image of having a positive, upbeat personality; hence she was seen primarily as a goddess of joy and love. Her sense of humor was renowned, as exemplified in the myth in which her divine father was upset after a heated argument with some other gods and retired into private to sulk. Determined to cheer him up, Hathor went to see him and while they

Hathor's Rampage

Although Hathor was usually viewed as a happy love goddess, she could also be very unhappy and destructive. In the so-called Myth of Cataclysm, she goes on a rampage and almost wipes out all of humanity.

were talking she suddenly yanked off her clothes and started dancing. This unexpected, audacious move made Ra erupt into a fit of laughter, erasing his former somber mood.

An ancient Egyptian papyrus depicts the falcon-headed sun god Ra sailing through the Underworld on his way to a new dawn above.

New Mythology for a New Nation

Like these tales of Ra and Hathor, most of ancient Egypt's myths told of the lives and exploits of various gods. This was partly because those deities stood at the center of the Egyptians' faith, which they practiced and perpetuated with extraordinary devotion and care. Modern experts are not completely sure

The Narmer Palette from 3000 B.C. depicts King Narmer slaying his enemies during his campaigns to unify Upper and Lower Egypt.

how that religion and its gods and attendant myths originated and developed. But they are fairly certain that initially the various deities were worshipped on the local level—that is, in separate villages, districts, and small kingdoms that existed well before Egypt became a unified nation. In those archaic times, each district might have its own creator-god, mother-goddess, deity of the dead, and so forth.

Possibly beginning around 6000 B.C. (eight thousand years ago), a slow but steady unification process began in the Nile Valley. As a result, after the passage of two thousand years or more, most of the villages and districts coalesced into two large rival kingdoms. One of them occupied so-called Lower Egypt. It stretched from the Nile Delta, bordering the southern shore of the Mediterranean Sea, down almost to the area where the city of Memphis was later built. The other kingdom, covering Upper Egypt, began in the Memphis area and continued down to Aswan, in the far south according to modern maps. (For the Egyptians, "upper" and "lower," referred to the direction of the Nile's flow. They saw its source—viewed as south today—as upper, and its delta—seen as north today—as lower.)

Each of the two large kingdoms still retained most of the local gods, myths, and religious customs that had accumulated within its borders for seemingly countless centuries. It would be quite confusing to the modern eye. The faith of each realm would seem like a bewildering jumble of hundreds of divinities, many of which duplicated others in form and function.

This unusual situation started to change somewhat in roughly 3100 B.C. A strong leader of Upper Egypt named Narmer (also known as Menes) unified the two lands, creating the world's first major nation-state. One of Narmer's great achievements was to bring together the many gods, beliefs, myths, and rituals of the north and south into a single religious structure. Local deities from near and far were organized into a hierarchy, or ladder of importance and authority. Those on the ladder's upper rungs were seen as major gods and the ones on the lower rungs were viewed as minor divinities.

At the same time, Narmer began construction on a new capital—Memphis—near the former border of the two lands and erected some large-scale temples to gods he viewed as particularly important. To these pivotal events, says Egyptologist Leonard H. Lesko, "almost all of

The Red and White Lands

The two kingdoms that united to form the Egyptian nation around 3100 B.C. are today sometimes called the Red Land and the White Land.

Egyptian mythology can be related in one way or another." This was because "existing mythology was recast and reemployed" by the government to explain those recent events, "and new mythology was produced for the same purpose." In the years that followed, Lesko continues, "local myths from throughout the country were brought together. [It is not certain] how long it took to create this national mythology, which sought to include almost every god and thereby to satisfy almost every person. It was a product of genius, however, and laid the foundation for one of the longest-lived civilizations in history."[12]

Classifying the Gods and Myths

Crucially and very shrewdly, when Narmer reorganized the structure of Egyptian religion, he did not rob some of his subjects of their traditional and beloved gods and myths. Rather, he used a decidedly inclusive approach. Deftly, he collected all of these elements into a sort of national religious melting pot. This is partly why thereafter the Egyptians had so many gods, along with numerous major and minor myths associated with them.

Still, there had to be a way to arrange the numerous gods and myths into types or groups for ease of recognition and worship. One way to categorize the gods was by their physical attributes. Some were viewed as having human form, while others were zoomorphs, or beings with the shape of animals, including lions, bulls, crocodiles, and falcons (or hawks). There were also bimorphs, or hybrids, that were part human and part animal.

Another way to classify various gods was by their function. Deities associated with agriculture and the soil's fertility were broadly admired, for example. This is not surprising considering that the vast majority of Egyptians were farmers. They recognized Geb as a deity of vegetation and Neper as a god who helped grain to grow. Meanwhile, the major god Osiris ensured the fertility of the soil and in one of his several myths taught humans the art of farming. In that story, he walked among the earliest Egyptians, just as his sister Isis had with her faithful scorpions. Osiris showed the region's first residents how to plow their fields, plant seeds, and harvest the mature crops, including wheat and barley. He also instructed people in how to grind these grains into flour and make bread. It is important to emphasize that the average Egyptian believed this myth was a memory of a real event. As such, it was one of the many examples of perpetuated myths serving the same function in ancient Egypt that history books serve in modern society.

The god Osiris ensured the fertility of the soil and taught humans the art of farming. He is depicted here as green, showing his function as the god of fertility.

Another common divine function was protection against evil or destructive forces. The god Kherty protected tombs, for example. This was seen as a vital job because the Egyptians believed a person's soul lived on for an undetermined period in his or her burial site. There were also protector gods of various professions, as well as of women and children. Of the latter deities, Taweret watched over women during childbirth and Harpokrates protected children from dangerous beasts.

Still another frequent grouping of Egyptian gods and myths contained those dealing with the creation and structure of the cosmos, or universe. It was thought that a vast, dark ocean filled the sky and stretched endlessly outward in all directions. Lying at the center of that infinite expanse of black water was a relatively dry dome- or bubble-shaped space. Inside the upper portion of that space rested the known world, with is fields, mountains, forests, rivers, animals, and people. Directly beneath the known world was the *Duat*, the region where the sun god Ra went at night in his most familiar myth. The Egyptians believed that the Underworld, the realm of the dead, lay somewhere inside the *Duat*.

The gods and their myths played key roles not only in the world's origins, but also in its very structure. In scholar James P. Allen's words, the Egyptians usually depicted the cosmos and earth "by using the mythological counterparts of its elements."[13] That is, they had myths that envisioned gods actually existing within and supporting the world's visible, physical sections.

For example, the goddess Nut's huge body arched over the top of the sky, holding back the dark, primeval waters lying beyond. Nut's divine father, Shu, god of air, stood below her, helping to keep her from falling. Meanwhile, Shu was supported beneath by the body of his son, Geb, who embodied the land. These myths also explained what are seen today as meteorological and geological phenomena. Rain, for instance, was depicted in a myth as the tears that Nut produced when she cried. Similarly, earthquakes occurred from the vibrations caused by Geb's hearty laughter.

The Rituals of Faith

These many myths associated with the gods, as well as all aspects of Egyptian life, were perpetuated in several ways. Paintings on the walls of tombs, palaces, and temples was one way. Another consisted of inscriptions made on stone monuments and in scrolls (rolls of paper made from the papyrus plant) after writing was introduced shortly before 3000 B.C. The principal method, however, employed both before and after the Egyptians adopted writing, was oral transmission, or word of mouth. Roving storytellers and ordinary people told and retold these special stories, passing them on to each succeeding generation.

The key storytellers, however, were the priests who ran the temples dedicated to the various gods. Unlike their modern counterparts, Egyptian priests were not full-time spiritual guides who oversaw congregations of worshippers and gave them advice on how to lead decent lives. Rather, most priests in ancient Egypt tended the temples and the sacred statues of the gods residing inside them. In addition, the priests collected and passed on the myths associated with the gods they represented. This was how the Greek historian Herodotus learned about the events and figures of Egypt's past when he visited the country in the fifth century B.C. Most of these "historical chronicles" the curious Greek absorbed and wrote about were actually myths, including the one that told how the creator god Amun's oracles spread from Egypt to Libya and Greece.

The priests were also in charge of another crucial religious ritual relating to the gods and myths—sacrifice. In the ancient world, sacrifices were material offerings made to a god or gods. Most often they took the form of some kind of nourishment, including animal meat; grains and other crops; and liquids, milk and wine being favorites. Herodotus witnessed some Egyptian sacrifices in which animals were ritually slaughtered and parts of the carcasses were burned. It was believed that the smoke from the burning animal rose up and nourished the god for whom the sacrifice was intended.

The Emergence of Writing

The Egyptians' first writing system, consisting of a series of little pictures known as hieroglyphics (from the Greek for "sacred signs") emerged around 3200 B.C.

The Nile's Annual Miracle

In this excerpt from his popular history of ancient Egypt, English historian Toby Wilkinson describes the yearly Nile flooding and its importance to Egyptian society.

The Nile performed an annual miracle. The summer rains falling over the Ethiopian highlands [situated well south of Egypt] swelled the [Nile], sending a torrent of water downstream (in this case north). By early August the approaching inundation was clearly discernible in the far south of Egypt, [and] a few days later, the flood arrived in earnest. With an unstoppable force, the Nile burst its banks, and the waters spread out over the floodplain . . . along the entire length of the Nile Valley. For several weeks, all the cultivable land was underwater. But as well as destruction, the inundation brought with it the potential for new life. [For] once the flood retreated, the soil emerged again, fertilized and irrigated, ready for the sowing of crops. It was thanks to this annual phenomenon that Egypt enjoyed such productive agriculture.

Toby Wilkinson. *The Rise and Fall of Ancient Egypt.* New York: Random House, 2010, pp. 15–16.

A mural from the twenty-third century B.C. shows the annual flooding of the Nile that made farming possible.

An Egyptian wall painting depicts the sacred symbol known as the eye of Horus, which warded off evil and protected the wearer.

Herodotus also saw how the priests followed strict rules during all stages of the sacrificial ritual. Before offering up a bull, for instance, "A priest appointed for the purpose examines the animal [with] the greatest care, first making him stand up, then lie on his back."[14] In another common ritual of the Egyptian faith, a priest said to the victim (the animal being sacrificed), "I bring you the Eye of Horus."[15]

This phrase referred to the most famous of the several myths in which sacrifices to the gods played a role. In that story, before humans were created, Ra ruled over the other gods on earth. When he finally decided he was tired of his job, the other deities fought among themselves to determine who would be their new leader. Eventually only two were left standing—Horus and his uncle Seth, who proceeded to fight. At one point Seth snatched out his nephew's eye, and in retaliation Horus badly injured Seth. As the two gods lay on the ground moaning, Thoth, deity of knowledge and wisdom, came over and offered to heal them with his powerful magic. The word he spoke to effect the healing was *hotep*, meaning "an offering." In this case, it was a peace offering, but that word could also denote the offerings people made to gods. So thereafter, every time an Egyptian performed a sacrifice, he reenacted Thoth's offering by saying, "I bring you the eye of Horus."

In the Realm of the Dead

Still another way that myths were intertwined with Egyptian religious beliefs was in people's expectations about the afterlife. Because the residents of ancient Egypt were so devoutly religious, they were absolutely convinced that an afterlife and realm of the dead existed. As a result, they allocated a great deal of their daily and yearly thoughts and energies to what the afterlife would be like and how to prepare for it. Indeed, Egyptologist Bob Brier notes, "No civilization ever

In a scene from the Book of the Dead, a person is judged at the court of Osiris to determine whether he is worthy enough to enter eternal life or be punished with horrible tortures.

devoted so much of its energies and resources to the quest for immortality as did Egypt's."[16]

As in so many other areas of Egyptian life, common myths helped people to understand what to expect in the afterlife. There were stories and legends about what the soul experienced soon after crossing the mysterious border between life and death, for example. The most important initial event was the judgment of the dead. It decided whether the person's essence would proceed into the great beyond for eternity or be punished through horrible tortures and utter destruction. The person's soul appeared before Osiris, lord of the Underworld, and a panel of grim supernatural judges who assisted him. They determined whether the person had led an ethical enough life to warrant eternal life.

If the judges felt the individual was *not* worthy of going any further, they tossed the unfortunate soul to a dreadful demon known as the "Swallower of the Damned." It promptly tore the soul to shreds and, as the monster's name suggests, gulped it down. In contrast, if the judges gave the soul a pass, myths foretold a number of possible outcomes. In the most common one, the life of the soul more or less duplicated that which the person had led on earth. A man who had been a farmer remained a farmer in the afterlife, therefore, with much the same daily tasks and duties. The main difference, which Egyptians found consoling, was that they would experience no cruelty, pain, or suffering in the world beyond.

In this way, myths and legends provided the ancient Egyptians with a kind of framework that supported and guided them in their actions and in their thinking about both life and death.

CHAPTER 2

Mythical Accounts of the Creation

Long before the creation of humans and their civilization, chaos was all that existed. Dark, moist, and seemingly limitless, it was like a vast, featureless ocean having no shores, surface, or bottom. Later, when the Egyptians appeared on the scene, they called that primeval, formless sea Nun and worshipped him as the first god. They believed that Nun existed, alone and silent, for untold eons, until suddenly a second deity—Atum, who would become the king of the gods—somehow sprang from the blackness that was Nun's body.

Wasting no time, Atum, the great creator, spoke. As he produced the first words ever heard, the explosion of his incredibly loud voice set the rest of creation in motion and he began to fashion other gods. Then from his own body he made the first patch of dry land—the sacred *benben*—and in its center he placed the first city, blessed Thebes. Finally, the astounding Atum rose into the sky and became the mighty sun god, Atum-Ra.

An Underlying Unity and Harmony

So went one of the four major cosmogonies, or creation myths, of ancient Egypt. There were also several minor ones, and a number of them contradicted one another in various ways. The reason for this can be seen in Narmer's unification of religious beliefs from various parts of the country in about 3100 B.C. Each separate region developed its personal patron gods and creation stories, which became deeply embedded in local tradition. Narmer smartly refrained from choosing one for the country as a whole. Instead, he perpetuated the multiple creation traditions in order to satisfy people from all parts of the new nation and thereby maintain their obedience and support.

To many people today, who are used to their religion having a single, definitive creation tale, the idea of a faith having several such stories seems strange and disconcerting. But the Egyptians came to accept all of these myths as equally valid, in spite of the inconsistencies among them.

The god Atum sits to the right of Osiris in this bas-relief. Atum rose into the sky and became Atum-Ra, the sun god.

This is largely because people did not view the stories as strictly literal accounts, with one being more factual than another. Rather they saw them more as mystical and symbolic in nature and thereby containing concepts the human intellect could not completely comprehend. That gave the tales a strong aura of awe and mystery that the Egyptians found compelling. Also, despite their differences, the various cosmogonies had an important factor in common. Namely, they all emphasized the importance of order and continuity in the universe. That gave people the comforting feeling that their nation, culture, and social order would always be stable and secure.

The Narmer Palette depicts two mythical beasts representing Upper and Lower Egypt that have combined into one nation. Narmer kept the creation myths of both regions as a way of unifying the people.

An appropriate modern parallel would be how all modern Christians accept the authority of the four Gospels (of Matthew, Mark, Luke, and John) in the Bible's New Testament. These stories of Jesus's life and preaching vary and contradict one another in several of their details. Yet to Christians, all four are equally legitimate and sacred in that they are differing versions of a larger, underlying truth. Similarly, the ancient Egyptians saw a universal truth beneath the details of their own conflicting creation stories. In the words of historian Vincent A. Tobin, all of these creation myths "bore witness to the unity, harmony, and singleness of everything that exists."[17]

Egypt at the Center of Things?

The Egyptians' mythical tales of creation also gave them an appreciation for where they stood in the known world. Not only was Egypt in the geographical center of things, they believed, but also its inhabitants were superior to other peoples. The supposed evidence for these contentions could be found in the creation stories. First, these myths claimed that the Nile Valley had been the very focal point of creation. This imparted to the Egyptians an exaggerated sense of their own importance in the world. After all, if they existed at the center of creation, the natural, cosmic order must revolve around them and their culture. They were therefore special to the gods, and, by extension, outsiders must be inferior, backward, irrelevant, or all of these things.

In this way, the Egyptian creation myths reinforced the purported uniqueness and natural supremacy of Egypt and its inhabitants. This explains why in their earliest centuries they ignored and remained more or less isolated from Palestine and Mesopotamia in the northeast and the rest of Africa in the south and southwest. During the Predynastic Period, the Egyptians simply had little interest in other peoples and nations, seeing them as lowly dwellers of the outer fringes of the civilized world.

The Heliopolitan Cosmogony

This alleged centrality of Egypt and its residents in the universal scheme of things was strongly reinforced by the most famous and influential of the culture's creation stories. It was the story of how the great god Atum emerged, of his own accord, from the murky, chaotic waters of Nun, the primeval ocean. "Heaven had not come into being," the god said in one of the *Pyramid Texts,* an anthology of religious writings dating from the 2300s B.C. or possibly earlier. "The earth had not come into being," Atum continued. With enormous strength and resolve, "I lifted myself from the watery mass." At that moment, "I was alone," but "I took courage in my heart. I laid a foundation."[18] That foundation consisted of setting all of creation in motion.

This fantastic tale derived from Heliopolis. Meaning "City of the Sun," it was the Greek (and in later ages most common) name for the Egyptian town Iunu, a key religious center located where Egypt's modern capital, Cairo, now stands. According to the ancient priests of Heliopolis, Atum was the monad—the original fountainhead, or source, from which the other gods sprang. The priests also claimed that when Atum fashioned the *benben,* or "mound of creation," that first piece of dry land rested in the very center of Heliopolis itself. So many Egyptians believed that Heliopolis lay at the center of the world.

Also, when Atum initially stood atop the sacred mound, he took the form of the mythical Bennu bird. Even when Atum assumed other forms, such as the sun god Atum-Ra, the story went, the holy Bennu remained as his inner soul. Although the blessed bird could no longer be seen in their day, the priests said, a small section of the original mound did remain. Inside the temple of Atum at Heliopolis, they kept close watch over it. According to ancient texts, it was a cone- or pyramid-shaped stone.

Most Egyptians never saw that special stone. Nor did the average person see the sacred images of the gods that stood within the inner chambers of the country's religious temples. This was because these buildings were not like modern churches—that is, places in which average people gather and worship. Instead, the interiors of Egyptian temples were secret abodes that were mostly restricted to priests and kings. Others, well-to-do and poor alike, were forbidden entry. Occasional religious ceremonies did take place in the

large, outer, open-air courtyards of some temples, but most Egyptians worshipped in their homes or fields or in gatherings in the streets during religious festivals.

Among the gods they prayed to were those that Atum created in the Heliopolitan myth—the twins Shu and Tefnut. They came from Atum's own bodily fluids, including saliva and semen. Soon after the two deities emerged, they proceeded to produce two more gods, Geb and Nut, who in their turn created four others—Isis, Osiris, Nephthys, and Seth (or Set). Together, Atum and the eight deities that developed from his fluids composed a highly revered group of nine divinities the Egyptians called the Ennead.

One Word with Many Meanings

The people of ancient Egypt recognized and worshipped hundreds of gods, and their concept of divine beings was both wide ranging and complex. This can be seen in their general word for "god"—*netcher*. It could mean a great and powerful deity, such as the popular mother goddess Isis, or her brother Osiris, ruler of the Underworld. Or it could be used to describe various minor deities with limited powers, such as Taweret, who watched over women during childbirth, or Mehen, a serpent god who protected the sun god. The word *netcher* also generally denoted dangerous or harmful supernatural beings, such as the demons and monsters that were thought to lurk in the Underworld. In addition, it could refer to humans (usually kings) who had been deified (given the status of a god) or even to ordinary dead people who returned to earth as ghosts.

After the Ennead had formed, the remainder of creation ensued. The mountains, valleys, plains, and other landforms arose. Then came the human race, which, like Shu, Tefnut, and their progeny, sprang initially from Atum's bodily fluids. In this case, his tears provided the magical ingredients of life. "Men and women arose from tears which came forth from my eye," the creator declared, as quoted in the *Pyramid Texts*. Finally, Atum made the animals and plants that existed on the land and in the seas. "I came forth from the plants," the deity recalled. "I created reptiles" and other beasts, "every form among them."[19]

The Politics of Creation

This great round of nonstop creation was accompanied by a powerful political component as well, a factor no doubt exploited to the utmost by pharaoh after pharaoh. It held that Atum was in essence the first king. So among his many feats of creation was the founding of Egypt's kingship and government. As Egyptologist Toby Wilkinson explains,

In Egyptian art, Atum was usually represented wearing the double crown of kingship, identifying him as the creator not just of the universe, but also of ancient Egypt's political system. The message was clear and unambiguous. If Atum was the first king as well as the first living being, then created order and political order were interdependent and inextricable [inseparable].[20]

That special relationship between Atum in this best-known creation myth and the pharaohs who sat on Egypt's throne was subtle yet important. It suggested that resistance to the king or his regime was equivalent to being against one of the most powerful and popular gods. In theory, therefore, someone who opposed the throne had more to fear than arrest by royal guards. That rebellious subject might be annihilated in some horrible manner by the god himself.

This partly explains why the vast majority of Egyptians, who were mostly poor farmers and other peasants, dutifully did the government's bidding for century after century. Because most of them were so religiously devout, their fear of divine wrath bred submission to authority. In turn, that compliance was frequently an effective deterrent against unruliness and revolt.

The Heliopolitan tale, along with other creation myths, encouraged the maintenance of social order among the Egyptians for another reason. These stories typically described ordered life emerging from chaos. Further, the average person was repeatedly exposed to that concept through hearing those myths told and retold beginning in early childhood. In spite of being chaotic, Wilkinson points out, Nun's dark primeval waters

> held within them the possibility of created order. This belief in the coexistence of opposites was characteristic of the Egyptian mind-set, and was deeply rooted in their distinctive geographical surroundings, [as, for example,] in the contrast between the arid desert and the fertile floodplain, and in the river itself, for the Nile could both create life and destroy it.[21]

A Fiery Glow at Hermopolis

Another major myth of beginnings emerged from the town of Hermopolis, lying roughly 150 miles (242km) south of Memphis, the capital Narmer had erected when he created the Egyptian nation. The Egyptians called Hermopolis (which was its Greek name) Khemnu. The latter meant "Town of the Eight," which referred to the eight gods who played key roles in the myths making up the so-called Hermopolitan cosmogony. The Egyptians referred to this set of eight deities as the sacred Ogdoad.

One crucial difference between the Heliopolitan and Hermopolitan mythological traditions was how they pictured where the earliest gods came from. In the creation story from Heliopolis, Nun gave rise to Atum, who then created other deities. In the Hermopolitan creation myth, by contrast, the members of the Ogdoad were not themselves created. Rather, in ways no one could explain, they already existed in the gloomy waters of the original universal ocean.

At first taking the bodily forms of snakes and frogs, these eight primal gods included Nun, Naunet, Hey, Hauhet, Kek, Kauket, Amun, and Amaunet. They existed in four pairs. For untold ages, according to the myth, the eight gods swam and swirled through the limitless primordial waters. Then, quite suddenly, they came together, and in so doing gave rise to the sun god Atum-Ra. At the same time, they produced the mound of creation (which the priests of Hermopolis claimed stood on the site of their own city, not at Heliopolis). In the colossal explosion of this burst of creation, writes former British Museum scholar George Hart, "the primeval mound was thrust clear." It became known as "the Isle of Flame because the sun-god was born on it and the cosmos witnessed the fiery glow of the first sunrise."[22]

The Hermopolitan concept of four pairs of deities was far from random. The priests who initially formulated it were aware that the number 4 had

Source of the Name Hermopolis

A number of Greek immigrants settled in the Egyptian town of Khemnu in the last few centuries B.C. They called it Hermopolis, meaning "city of Hermes," after the Greek god whom they equated with the Egyptian deity Thoth.

certain deep meanings in Egyptian society. The four cardinal points—north, south, east, and west—were viewed as important, for instance. People used them not only as aids in travel but also in observing the stars and other celestial bodies, as well as in laying out temples, palaces, and other large structures. The three huge pyramids at Giza (near modern Cairo) not only have four sides each but are also nearly perfectly aligned so that the sides of each structure point directly toward the four cardinal points. The reason for this is uncertain. But the fact that the number 4 stood for totality, or a system that was completed and in balance, may have had something to do with it.

The Egyptian obsession with the numbers 3, 4, and 5, the ratios of the sides of a right triangle, is illustrated by the Great Pyramids at Giza in whose creation Egyptian architects used right triangles.

Good at Math

The Egyptians were good at math, as demonstrated by the fact that they understood the ideas underlying the Pythagorean theorem at least a thousand years before the birth of the late sixth-century B.C. Greek thinker Pythagoras, after whom the concept was named.

Another reason the Egyptians saw the number 4 as exceptional was that it, along with two other special numbers, 3 and 5, formed the basis for the mathematical relationship later called the Pythagorean theorem. In modern terms, the three sides of a right triangle are frequently labeled a, b, and c. Often, a = 3, b = 4, and c = 5. When they are squared, or multiplied by themselves, one finds that $a^2 + b^2 = c^2$, or 9 (3 x 3) plus 16 (4 x 4) equals 25 (5 x 5). The Egyptians thought there was something mystical about this geometrical relationship; hence they associated the number 3 with the god Osiris, the number 4 with his sister and wife Isis, and the number 5 with their son, Horus. Moreover, Egyptian architects employed right triangles in creating several of the pyramids used as tombs for their kings. In the creation myth involving the Ogdoad, therefore, religious mysticism combined with mathematical mysticism, resulting in a spiritual vision that the Egyptians saw as powerful and compelling.

Creation by Miraculous Speech

A third major creation story came from Egypt's first national capital, Memphis. The star player in the Memphite tradition was Ptah, a deity long worshipped in that region as a protector of metalworkers and other craftspeople. Other elements in the tradition were the same as in the Heliopolitan creation story, including the nine-member Ennead, the god Atum, and the *benben*. A major difference, however, was that the Memphite myth claimed that Ptah existed *before* these other elements. In fact, Ptah was equated with Nun, the dark sky-ocean. Ptah/Nun gave rise to a daughter, Naunet, with whom he then mated and produced Atum.

More important than who created whom in the Memphite tradition was the matter of *how* Ptah created gods, the earth, animals, and so forth. He did it through the spoken word, so that when he named or verbally described something, it leapt into being out of the thin air. A damaged stone inscription from Memphis dating to the 700s B.C. describes this miraculous speech, saying that "there came into being from the heart and there came into being from the tongue ... the form of Atum." Further, "it is the tongue that repeats what the heart thinks. Thus all the gods were born," and creation "was completed through what the heart thought and the tongue commanded."[23]

Ptah's Creation Versus Biblical Creation

Modern scholars and other observers have looked closely at Ptah's use of vocal utterance as a tool of creation in the Memphite creation story. The god simply says certain words standing for various objects and these things suddenly appear, seemingly out of the thin air. This, these experts point out, is remarkably similar to the method of creation employed by the Judeo-Christian god in the Bible. A famous passage from the Bible's first book, Genesis, reads, "And God said, 'Let there be light'; and there was light."[1] Another biblical book, the Gospel of John, depicts the same episode, emphasizing the relationship between the act of speaking a word and the act of creation. The passage from John says, "In the beginning was the Word . . . and the Word was God."[2] Historian Vincent A. Tobin points out that "the Memphite tradition must be regarded as one of the more important products of the Egyptian mind because it [shows] that the Egyptian intellect was capable of dealing with material that would later form the subject of [intensive] theological speculation in the Jewish and Christian worlds."[3]

1. Genesis 1:3.
2. John 1:1.
3. Vincent A. Tobin. "Creations Myths." In *The Ancient Gods Speak: A Guide to Egyptian Religion*, edited by Donald B. Redford. New York: Oxford University Press, 2002, p. 249.

A tomb painting depicts the god Ptah. In the Memphite tradition, Ptah created all things through the spoken word.

These ancient words reflect the fact that the Egyptians had a completely incorrect notion of the heart's functions. At least in part because of what they heard in Ptah's creation tale and other myths, they believed that that organ, and not the brain, was the seat of thought, intelligence, memory, emotions, and even one's personality. In addition, people were convinced that the gods communicated with humans through the heart. Egypt possessed a relatively large collection of medical and surgical knowledge for an ancient society. Yet no one there realized that the heart is a pump that circulates blood through the body. Conversely, the actual seat of intelligence, the brain, was believed to be an unremarkable organ that transferred mucus to the nose. For these reasons, when the Egyptians mummified a deceased person, they summarily discarded the supposedly useless brain and made sure to keep what they thought was the all-powerful heart intact.

Crafting Humans from Clay

The last of the four major Egyptian creation myths developed much later than the others, during the New Kingdom. That period, lasting from 1550 to 1069 B.C., witnessed Egypt's expansion through the conquest of most of Palestine. Also during those years, Thebes, located on the Nile a few hundred miles south of Hermopolis, became the country's capital and most important city.

In and around Thebes, the priests of those local temples built to honor the god Amun developed their own version of how all things came to be. They held that this formerly minor member of the Ogdoad had a dual personality and role. He was not only a part of that eight-member divine unit, they said, but also, in the guise of Amun-Ra, the greatest of all gods.

Part of what made Amun so splendid, according to his worshippers, was that he had somehow predated the other members of the Ogdoad and gone on to create the world. When it came time to fashion the human race, however, Amun turned to another local deity from the region around Thebes—Khnum, most often depicted in art as a ram-headed man. Centuries before, Khnum had been pictured first as a

regulator of the Nile's annual floods and later as a master potter. But during the New Kingdom he rose in status to become a cocreator who aided Amun-Ra. Together, the two became known as the "Lords of Destiny."

After acquiring his assignment to create humans, Khnum found a special sort of clay on the Nile's banks and with it molded their bodies on his sturdy potter's wheel. Next, he inserted hearts, lungs, and other vital organs and then overlaid all with skin. Finally, Khnum breathed into these first people. That gave them part of his own life force and with it the ability to walk, think, and talk.

This myth of human beginnings proved instructive to the early Egyptians in several ways. One of the ways was as an inspiration for the potters who made bowls, cups, jugs, vases, dishes, wine jars, figurines, and numerous other practical, everyday, and largely inexpensive objects.

The special clay Khnum was said to have found on the riverbank and used to fashion the first human bodies was composed of nothing more than the Nile's silt. Over the course of years and centuries, the moving river waters carried and deposited tiny earthen particles, forming layers

During the New Kingdom the ram-headed god Khnum became a cocreator with Amun-Ra. It was Khnum who created humans out of clay.

Khnum Creates a Great Queen

As a divine potter, Khnum was often pictured creating not only human bodies but also the souls inhabiting those bodies. One Egyptian ruler of the New Kingdom shrewdly used that aspect of the Theban creation myth to enhance her royal image in the eyes of her subjects. She was Queen Hatshepsut (reigned 1473–1458 B.C.). In an inscription in one of her temples, she claimed that Khnum had created both her body and her soul, or ka. The inscription reads:

Amun-Ra called for Khnum, the creator, the fashioner of the bodies of men. "Fashion for me the body of my daughter and the body of her ka," said Amun-Ra. "A great queen shall I make of her, and honor and power shall be worthy of her dignity and glory." "O Amun-Ra," answered Khnum, "it shall be done as you have said. The beauty of your daughter shall surpass that of the gods and shall be worthy of her dignity and glory." So Khnum fashioned the body of Amen-Ra's daughter and the body of her ka, the two forms exactly alike and more beautiful than the daughters of men. He fashioned them of clay with the air of his potter's wheel and Heqet, goddess of birth, knelt by his side holding the sign of life towards the clay that the bodies of Hapshetsut and her ka might be filled with the breath of life.

Quoted in Caroline Seawright. "Khnum, Potter God of the Inundation Silt and Creation." www.touregypt.net/featurestories/khnum.htm.

of clay that grew increasingly deep and compact. Modern scholars call the pottery made from that clay "coarse ware" or "Nile silt ware."

Potters who produced coarse ware first prepared the clay by kneading it, most often by trampling it with their bare feet. Then a potter shaped the clay into the desired shape. For dozens of centuries this step was accomplished by hand. But eventually rudimentary potter's wheels were introduced, which made the work easier, faster, and produced a more symmetrical product. The next step was to air-dry the completed pot, after which the potter baked it in a kiln.

Unlike their role model, the creator god Khnum, Egyptian potters lacked the miraculous power to breathe life into their clay constructs. But they were thankful to that deity. Not only had he fashioned the human race, he had also introduced the occupation by which they made their mostly meager but necessary livings.

Similarly, with rare exceptions Egyptian professions, arts, and crafts of all kinds were thought to have been initially invented by gods, not humans. This was in keeping with the country's cherished creation myths. They consistently promoted the idea that originating something important was the province of the gods, not of subservient humanity, which had itself been devised by those divinities.

CHAPTER 3

Osiris, Isis, and the Myth of Kingship

A trinity of gods—made up of Osiris, Isis, and Horus—who also formed a divine family unit, were the principal players in the most famous and important of all ancient Egyptian myths. It was the dark, at times suspenseful, and ultimately inspiring story of Osiris's murder and subsequent resurrection. Because that tale had crucial spiritual, political, and social implications, it was in a very real sense a vital guiding force in Egyptian life.

Spiritually speaking, the myth lay at the very heart of the Egyptians' religious faith. In this respect, in fact, it parallels the way another resurrection story—that of Jesus of Nazareth—is central to the Christian faith. Jesus's return from death is thought to bring salvation to Christians in the afterlife. Similarly, Osiris's restoration and his assumption of the role of ruler of the land of the dead were seen as assurances that ordinary Egyptians would have a chance to dwell in that land for eternity.

Osiris's rebirth had potent political consequences as well. At least by the time of the late Old Kingdom (ca. 2400–2200 B.C.), each deceased pharaoh was identified with that deity. Indeed, people went so far as to think that the dead king had become one with Osiris, taking on his divine spirit and abilities.

At the same time, the events of the myth supposedly established that the new pharaoh had become one with Osiris's son, Horus. It was seen as essential that there be a living link between the gods and humans, and only the king had sufficient status and clout to fulfill that role. Egyptologist Rosalie David explains,

> As the incarnation [flesh-and-blood form] of the god Horus, and the son of Ra and divine heir, only [the pharaoh] could act as mankind's agent in the presence of the gods. The Egyptians considered the rituals to be effective only if they were enacted by the king to whom the gods had given the rulerships. Only he could attend to their needs and execute their orders.[24]

Because of these critical connections to the office of pharaoh, this highly influential tale became known as the Myth of Kingship.

The Central Characters

Even before the Myth of Kingship became popular and indispensable to Egyptian worship, its central character, Osiris, was viewed as an important fertility god. It was thought that he made the Nile flood each year, which brought life and prosperity to humanity. In the very archaic myth in which he walked among humans and taught them how to farm, he also instructed them in the digging of irrigation ditches and canals. In that same tale, moreover, Osiris built dams and floodgates to help control the rising waters. Supposedly, these acts made it possible for the early Egyptians to grow enough food to sustain themselves and survive. This was and remains one of the more vivid examples of how the contents of a myth affected the thinking and everyday lives of the people who perpetuated that tale. The Nile, Toby Wilkinson points out, "molds not only the physical landscape" of Egypt,

> but also the way in which the Egyptians think about themselves and their place in the world. The landscape has influenced their habits and customs, and from an early period it imprinted itself upon their collective psyche, shaping over the course of generations their most fundamental philosophical and religious beliefs.[25]

Because Osiris controlled the influx of Nile waters and sponsored farming, he was, by default, a promoter of fertile soil, which was crucial to crops' growth and maturation. Like all other life forms, crops came and went in a cycle of death and renewal. Through his death and resurrection in the Myth of Kingship, Osiris elevated that same theme to a more dramatic level that all Egyptians found compelling. They perceived the myth as by far the most splendid example of the eternal death-and-rebirth cycle in the natural world. It is no wonder, therefore, that this theme became one of the pillars of the Egyptian faith.

The second major character in the myth of kingship was Osiris's sister, Isis, who also became his wife. In another example of myths strongly influencing Egyptian life and cus-

Gold and lapis lazuli figures of (from left to right) Isis, Horus, and Osiris, the main players in the Myth of Kingship.

toms, the marriage of these two sibling deities became the model for marital unions between royal brothers and sisters. The practice became fairly common during the New Kingdom and later Egyptian times.

Like Osiris, Isis helped to ensure the fertility of the soil. She became especially associated with wheat and barley, two grain crops that made Egypt one of Mediterranean civilization's key breadbaskets throughout most of ancient times. Isis was also widely known as a kind, nurturing, bighearted mother, not only to Horus, but to humanity, too. It was said that she listened to the prayers of slaves and sinners as well as those of wealthy and noble people. In addition, as demonstrated in the myth in which she healed a child stung by giant scorpions, Isis possessed potent magical abilities.

A detailed description of Isis, as she was seen in the first millennium B.C., appears in *The Golden Ass,* a surviving novel by the Roman writer Apuleius. "Her lofty head was encircled by a garland interwoven with diverse blossoms," it says, describing an image of the goddess in a religious procession. At the center of this floral bouquet,

> was a flat disk resembling a mirror, or rather the orb of the moon, which emitted a glittering light. The crown was held in place by coils of rearing snakes [and] adorned above with waving ears of corn. She wore a multicolored dress woven from fine linen, one part of which shone radiantly white, a second glowed yellow with saffron blossom, and a third blazed rosy red.[26]

A third major player in the myth, Horus, was frequently depicted as a sky god, like the sun god Ra. In fact, one early myth said that Horus, whom artists often portrayed as a falcon, flew across the sky each day, carrying the sun in one eye socket and the moon in the other. Also, as Isis's beloved son, Horus was frequently viewed as a beautiful,

Depictions of Osiris

In ancient Egypt, Osiris, lord of the Underworld, was most often depicted in paintings and other visual representations as a mummy wrapped in bandages and holding the chief insignia of Egyptian royalty—the crook and the flail.

radiant infant, much like the baby Jesus in Christian lore. Horus was a benevolent god. As such, he projected an image nearly opposite to that of his divine uncle—Seth, the fourth leading character in the myth of kingship. A deity of the desert and storms, that brother to Osiris and Isis was variously seen as dark, irritable, and at times even mean and cruel.

Death and Transfiguration

Seth was certainly mean-spirited in the Myth of Kingship, in which his petty jealousy for his brother set the story's chief events in motion. Back in the days when Osiris was showing the early Egyptians how to plant and harvest their crops, the tale went, he also ruled them as their king. The wise and gracious Isis, in the role of Egypt's queen, assisted him. The people, who were thriving and happy, loved and respected these divine monarchs and lavished praises on them on a regular basis.

Meanwhile, the envious Seth hated that his brother received so much adulation and little by little formulated a plan to kill him and seize the throne for himself. The storm-god decided to strike on a night when Isis was away and the king was throwing a sumptuous banquet at the palace. Seth arrived carrying a large, lavishly decorated treasure chest. He challenged Osiris and his guests to take turns lying inside the chest, and said that whoever fit in it the best would be allowed to keep it.

One by one, the partiers took their turns climbing into the chest. But just as Seth had planned in advance, only Osiris made the perfect fit, and while the king reclined inside the handsome box, his brother suddenly shut and locked it, trapping Osiris inside. The pharaoh soon suffocated to death from lack of air, after which Seth and his henchmen took the chest to the Nile and tossed it in. Then Seth proclaimed himself Egypt's new pharaoh and made it known that he would not be the irritating do-gooder his brother had been.

Not long after the royal murder had transpired, Isis returned to the capital and found out what had happened. She was quite naturally surprised and grief stricken. But she wasted no time in launching a desperate search for her husband's remains. Managing to find the chest at the bottom of the river, she hid it in some desolate marshes, hoping to keep Seth from finding it and taking the body away from her. However, while out hunting, the new king did come upon the chest. In a fit of rage he cut Osiris's body into thousands of pieces. Seth then told his corrupt helpers to spread them from one end of Egypt to the other.

What Seth had not counted on was the depth of his sister's love for her husband, as well as her sheer will and determination. Isis searched night and day for many years until she had found all the pieces of Osiris's corpse. Carefully and lovingly, she reassembled them. Then, employing

The falcon-headed god Horus was generally viewed as a benevolent god.

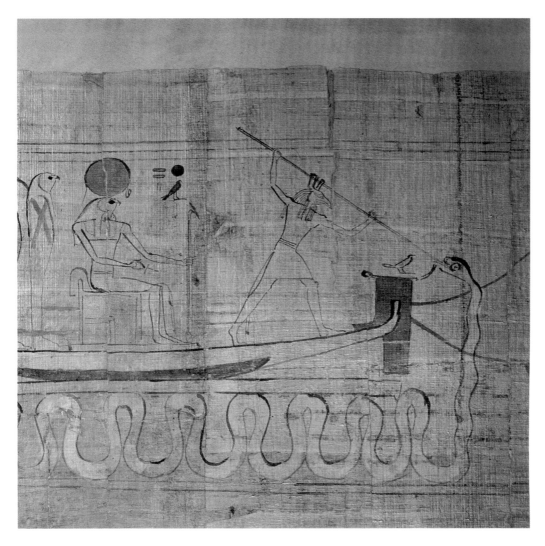

This papyrus drawing depicts the god Seth killing the serpent Apophis from the sun boat. Seth is also known for killing his brother Osiris, whom Isis then brought back to life.

a series of magical spells, she transfigured her husband, or brought him back to life. The two were overjoyed at seeing each other again. Soon thereafter they conceived a child, the heroic Horus.

Democracy in the Afterlife?

At the conclusion of this first half of the Myth of Kingship, the great god Ra called on Osiris to leave Egypt and the world of people behind and become ruler of the Underworld. Osiris had taught humans a great deal about how to maintain their lives on earth, Ra said. Now, it was time for him to help them in the realm they would go to when their lives were over. As a result, the average Egyptian no longer feared death because he knew that Osiris would look after his soul in the realm of the dead.

It is important to emphasize that this was *not* the way most Egyptians pictured their afterlife existence before the Myth of Kingship fully developed in the late 2000s B.C. Evidence indicates that in earlier times the general view was that only the pharaoh enjoyed the gift of immortality in the afterlife. A few other people—those who closely attended him in his life, including his wives, leading advisers, and servants—might make it to the afterlife because he required their aid to sustain himself there. But it was thought that every other Egyptian was barred from the benefits of life after death. When they died, they simply rotted away and passed into oblivion.

With the ascendancy of the Myth of Kingship, however, in which Osiris rose to the status of lord of the Underworld, those older, very undemocratic beliefs quickly faded away.

Forcing Substitute Laborers to Work

The surfaces of shawabtis, *the small statues that some Egyptians put in their tombs in hopes that these substitute workers would perform labor for them in the afterlife, most often had writing on them. Some bore the name of the person who had died. It was also common to inscribe a spell that it was thought would force the statuette to do the work it was intended to accomplish in Osiris's kingdom. Following is such a spell, discovered by archaeologists on a* shawabti *in the grave of a man named Setau, who was buried during the reign of the New Kingdom pharaoh Akhenaten.*

The servant in the Place of Truth, Setau, justified, says: Oh, this *shawabti*! If one [expects] Setau, justified, to do any work which is done [in the afterlife]—now indeed an obligation has been set up for him there, as a man at his duties, to cultivate the fields, to irrigate the [farmlands], to transport the sand from [one place to another]—if you [the *shawabti*] are called at any time [to do such work], "Here I am!" you shall say.

Quoted in A.G. McDowall. *Village Life in Ancient Egypt.* New York: Oxford University Press, 1999, p. 120.

The newly invigorated Osiris brought salvation for all people, even the poor, as long as he and his judges determined they were worthy. If a person did manage to make it past those subterranean judges, people believed, they entered not a paradise, as envisioned in the heaven of Christians and Muslims, but a place very much like the one they had just left. Osiris's kingdom in the Underworld, David writes,

> was envisioned as a place of lush vegetation, a mirror image of the cultivated land of Egypt, that was situated somewhere below the western horizon or on a group of islands. This kingdom is sometimes called the "Field of Reeds," and the inhabitants were believed to enjoy eternal springtime, unfailing harvests, and no pain or suffering. The land was democratically divided into equal plots that rich and poor alike were expected to cultivate.[27]

Most Egyptians welcomed these democratic notions about equality in the afterlife. This is hardly surprising considering that in their present lives the vast majority of them were destitute and lacking in creature comforts. The concept of all people having to fend for themselves in the next life did not go over so well with Egypt's wealthy and important citizens, however. As belief in Osiris's underground kingdom steadily took hold, the rich searched for some way they could avoid having to work like ordinary people in the afterlife.

Figurines with Accessories

The figurines called *shawabtis*, which were thought to become farmers in the afterlife, were often accompanied by miniature hoes and other farm tools—and at times even with models of overseers brandishing whips.

This was how the custom of placing *shawabtis* (or *shabtis*, or *ushabtis*) in tombs came about. When modern archaeologists began excavating the tombs of the nobles and other wealthy folk of ancient Egypt, they found dozens and sometimes hundreds of these human-shaped figurines in each tomb. The belief was that the small statues would magically come to life and perform the menial labor required of the dead person's soul in the afterlife. "The deceased would have to plant the fields and maintain irrigation canals,"

says noted scholar Bob Brier, "so the little statues buried in tombs began to look more like field workers than mummies." They still had the general look of mummies, which was the standard burial custom, "but their hands were shown protruding from the bandages so as to be able to do work."[28]

Battling for the Throne

The second half of the Myth of Kingship had major consequences for society in the present life rather than in the afterlife. This part of the story dealt with the adult Horus's efforts to exact revenge on Seth for murdering Osiris. After scattering the pieces of his brother's body, Seth planned on ruling Egypt as a stern dictator virtually forever. He did not

Ancient Egyptians placed shawabtis, *or human-shaped figurines, in the graves of the rich. These figurines were thought to perform menial labors for the deceased in the afterlife.*

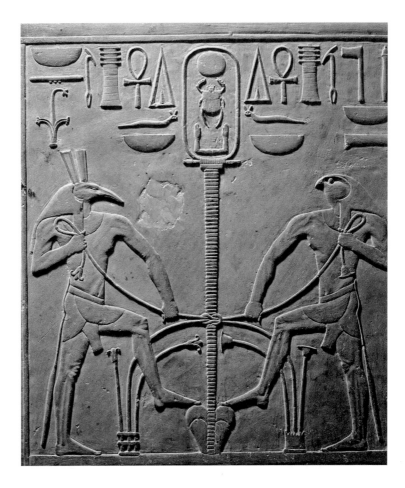

The gods Seth (left) and Horus would battle for the throne of Egypt.

foresee the birth of Horus or the latter's steadfast campaign to avenge the wrongs his uncle had committed.

That campaign began when Horus called together the deities making up the sacred Ennead, along with some other gods, and asked them to back his bid for the Egyptian throne. After he had recalled Seth's crimes and made his claim, the other divine beings agreed that he had made a good case. He should replace Seth as Egypt's pharaoh, they said.

When Seth heard about the meeting, he was enraged and boldly threatened the other gods who had agreed to back Horus's claim. Loudly shouting, Seth said he would use his kingly scepter as a club and beat to death one deity per day until the survivors reversed themselves and rejected Horus's bid for the throne. Threatening the other

Hathor Heals Horus

During the battle between Horus and Seth in the Myth of Kingship, the two gods battled off and on for many days. At one point during a break in the conflict, Horus was resting under a tree in a desert oasis, when suddenly Seth appeared and assaulted him. Seth "seized hold of him," says a second-millennium B.C. document titled *The Contendings of Horus and Seth.* He "threw him down upon his back on the mountain, removed his two eyes from their sockets, and buried them on the mountain." Seth then departed, laughing, because he assumed that he had won the war with his nephew. But all was not lost for Horus. A while later, the bovine goddess Hathor "found Horus lying weeping in the desert. She captured a gazelle and milked it. She said to Horus, 'Open your eyes so that I may put this milk into them.'" Horus did as she instructed and soon found to his relief that he had been healed.

Quoted in William K. Simpson, ed. *The Literature of Ancient Egypt: An Anthology of Stories, Instructions, and Poetry.* New Haven, CT: Yale University Press, 2003, p. 119.

A detail from the Book of the Dead *depicts the goddess Hathor in her cow form presenting a noblewoman with the eye of Horus.*

gods was a mistake on Seth's part. Ignoring his bluster, they went ahead and voted to make Horus king. According to a text dating from around 2000 B.C., those divinities placed Egypt's crown on Horus's head, "and he was installed in the [former] position of his father, Osiris. He was told: 'You are a good king of Egypt. You are the good lord of every land unto all eternity.' Thereupon Isis let out a loud shriek [of joy] on behalf of her son Horus, saying, 'You are the good king! My heart is in joy.'"[29]

Now more angry than ever, Seth refused to accept what his fellow gods had done. He furiously challenged Horus to a fight to the death for possession of the throne, and Isis's son accepted. As the other deities looked on, the two irate gods clashed in a series of epic battles. In one, they took the form of enormous, dangerous hippos and thrashed about for hours in the Nile's deepest waters. Later, after they had retaken their normal forms, Seth ripped out Horus's eyes. But fortunately for the younger god, the goddess Hathor intervened and restored his sight.

Finally, none other than the mighty Osiris, the recently established ruler of the Underworld, appeared on the scene. He reminded Seth that many horrifying serpents, monsters, and other "savage-faced messengers who do not fear any god"[30] dwelled in the darkest reaches of the Underworld. These frightening beasts now did Osiris's bidding, he warned, and he would unleash them on Seth if he did not allow Horus to remain king. Hearing this, Seth became fearful and relented, and for a long time afterward Horus sat on Egypt's throne.

The Culture Reshaped

According to mythical tradition, Horus was the last god to rule Egypt. He eventually passed the kingship on to a line of human kings, who, it was thought, possessed some divine sparks because of their connections with him. Each of these pharaohs *was* Horus in the symbolic sense as long as he lived and ruled. But after a pharaoh's passing, he became, symbolically, Osiris, who oversaw and protected the souls of kings.

These beliefs based on the Myth of Kingship affected the manner in which the highest level of the country's government operated, as well as how people depicted the gods and pharaoh in art. In regard to the king himself, for instance, certain aspects of the myth were reflected in one of the several official names each pharaoh bore, known as the *nesu-bit* name. The term *nesu* signified the kingship itself, which was viewed as a divine creation. The word *bit* described the current king. "Each king," as Egyptologist Ian Shaw tells it, "was therefore a combination of the divine and the mortal [in] the same way that the living king was linked with Horus, and the dead kings, the royal ancestors, were associated with Horus's father Osiris."[31]

Also, this belief that the pharaohs were semidivine manifestations of Horus and Osiris generated other customs

A pharaoh appears before Osiris, Isis, Ma'at, and Horus. Pharaohs were believed to be semidivine manifestations of Horus and Osiris and deserving of worship.

surrounding Egypt's throne. If past pharaohs were indeed embodiments of gods, the thinking went, then they deserved to be worshipped. So as the nation increasingly embraced the Myth of Kingship, the government began the tradition of venerating the king's ancestors with prayers and sacrifices.

In turn, it was seen as necessary to keep an accurate record of the royal ancestors. That would hopefully ensure that none of them were offended by a failure to give them their due worship. This record of past pharaohs came to be called the "king lists," a catalog of names of those who had sat on the throne. The lists were inscribed on the walls of tombs and temples, written on papyrus rolls, and carved onto large rocks in the desert. A few versions have survived, which have helped modern scholars in their efforts to understand the succession of Egypt's kings.

Of the other social customs inspired by the Myth of Kingship, particularly striking are a number of artistic and cultural conventions. For example, dramatic or colorful moments from the battle between Horus and Seth became favorite subjects of painters. Especially popular were renderings of the two gods as frantically wrestling hippos.

There was also a theatrical play performed each year at Edfu, a town on the Nile several miles south of Thebes. Part of a religious celebration called the Festival of Victory, it featured actors in elaborate costumes representing Isis, Horus, and Seth. They re-created the epic encounter between the Horus-hippo and Seth-hippo. At the end of the festival, worshippers ate cakes made from hippo parts to commemorate brave Horus's victory over his dastardly uncle.

These were only some of the ways that the Egyptians memorialized their favorite myth. In the process, their religious and social customs, art, and literature, along with the way they viewed their kings, were forever reshaped.

CHAPTER **4**

Myths Based on Real Characters

Not all Egyptian myths depicted the creation, exploits, and problems of the gods that the people of Egypt so reverently worshipped. Mythical tales of the experiences and adventures of human beings were also popular, although these characters were most often far from ordinary. As a rule, they were gifted with unusual intelligence or shrewdness, or uncommon daring or bravery, or the good fortune to be in an opportune situation at just the right time.

Egyptian mythology was therefore well supplied with legendary heroes, geniuses, rascals, and adventurers. Their myths were often lighthearted, amusing, and/or engaging. So they filled a needed niche in the lives of most Egyptians. Like all other peoples in history, Egyptians felt the normal human craving for occasional diversions or entertainment that might take their minds off their troubles or mundane daily routines.

At least one character in each of these tales was an actual person of a past age. For instance, the real New Kingdom pharaoh Ramesses II appeared in several myths that developed centuries after his reign, among them one sometimes called "The Princess and the Demon." Similarly, evidence indicates that another, even earlier mythical human hero— a man who was later accorded the status of a god—was a real person as well. Named Imhotep, he was an adviser and architect to at least two different pharaohs during the 2600s B.C. Imhotep was so talented and accomplished that he became a legend not only in his own time but also for all time. As the centuries rolled by, his abilities and deeds became more and more esteemed or exaggerated, until finally people assumed that no ordinary human could have done what he did; he had to have been a god.

To one degree or another, other legendary Egyptian characters, among them the military hero General Djehuty and the resourceful wanderer Sinuhe, gained mythical status. Partly because the United States is less than three centuries old (and also because modern historians have kept detailed records), not enough time has elapsed for U.S. presidents George Washington or John Adams, for example, to be accorded such special standing. In contrast, ancient Egyptian civilization lasted for thousands of years. So there was plenty of time for some real people in earlier eras to be transformed into mythical figures in later ages.

Architect of the First Pyramid

This is precisely what occurred in the case of Imhotep. He served as vizier, or chief administrator, to Djoser, the second pharaoh of the Old Kingdom (reigned 2667–2648 B.C.). A brilliant and multitalented individual, Imhotep was an architect, philosopher, high priest of the sun god Ra, and possibly a physician who wrote an important medical treatise. In addition, scholar George Hart writes, Imhotep's "reputation as an experienced architect led to his adoption by the scribes of Egypt as the most eminent practitioner of their craft. He became regarded as a source of intellectual inspiration and a number of moral maxims were alleged to have been committed to papyrus in his name."[32]

Imhotep's greatest achievement in life was designing and overseeing construction of Egypt's first pyramid-tomb,

Origin of the Term Mastaba

The term *mastaba* comes from an Egyptian word meaning "bench." This was because mastabas looked a lot like the simple wooden benches that rested near the front doors of most Egyptian homes.

Imhotep was an architect, philosopher, priest, and the builder of the first pyramid, which was for the pharaoh Djoser.

the Step Pyramid at Saqqara (just north of Memphis). Before his time, deceased Egyptian royalty and nobility had been buried in tombs called mastabas, which were one-story, flat-topped structures initially constructed of sun-dried mud bricks. Over time, they came to be seen as less and less useful, partly because the unstable bricks deteriorated rapidly, necessitating frequent repairs. They also proved vulnerable to the tools of tomb robbers. So in the early years of the Old Kingdom, builders began to employ stone for mastabas.

That improvement gave Imhotep, who was about to start work on King Djoser's tomb, a novel idea. The royal architect decided to stack six stone mastabas on top of one another, each one slightly smaller than the one beneath it, thereby creating a pyramid. Because each of the levels is recessed inward several feet from the one below it, they look like big steps, from which the structure got its name. In its prime, Djoser's pyramid was 413 feet (126m) long and 344 feet (105m) wide at its base and rose to a height of about 200 feet (61m).

Following Imhotep's death, his reputation not only survived but actually increased over the course of many cen-

Djoser's pyramid at Saqqara was designed by Imhotep.

turies. Eventually, various minor myths arose about him, including one in which Ptah, the creator god of Memphis, brought about Imhotep's birth as Ptah's own son. Later, in the 600s B.C., two full millennia after his death, the Egyptians deified Imhotep, or recognized him as a god. This confirmed his place in the mythical divine realm. After that, people identified him with Thoth, the god who was patron of scribes and oversaw medicine and architecture. Imhotep also had a temple dedicated to him in Saqqara, where his step pyramid was (and remains today). In the years that followed, a myth evolved in which he appeared in a woman's dream and promised to help her become pregnant and bear a son, which supposedly she did.

The Capture of Joppa

Another real-life Egyptian raised to mythic status was a hero of a different sort. General Djehuty (also known as Thot or Thuti) served as one of the top military commanders of the New Kingdom pharaoh Tuthmosis III (reigned 1479–1425 B.C.). The evidence that Djehuty actually existed lies in his personal remains, found in his undisturbed tomb at Saqqara in 1824.

In life, Djehuty helped in Tuthmosis's conquest of parts of Palestine and Syria. The general's specific accomplishments in these campaigns are uncertain, but in later centuries a legend developed about how he captured the city of Joppa (modern Jaffa), on Palestine's coast.

The main version of the myth appears on a papyrus now on display in the British Museum.

In the story, Tuthmosis ordered Djehuty to conquer Joppa, and the general decided to use a strategy of stealth rather than standard siege techniques. First, the cunning general surrounded the city but refrained from attacking it for more than a week. Then he sent a messenger to the prince of Joppa. On Djehuty's orders, the courier claimed that the Egyptian forces were low on food and in disarray and that General Djehuty had decided to give up. Moreover, as a peace offering the general would send several hundred unarmed men into Joppa. These envoys would be carrying big wicker baskets filled with gifts for the city's inhabitants. Thrilled at having avoided a siege and untold bloodshed and death, the prince told the messenger that he accepted the deal.

What the prince did not know was that the baskets did not contain gifts. Rather, Djehuty slyly placed some of his best soldiers, all heavily armed, inside the baskets. Then he told the basket carriers, "When you enter the city, you are to let out your companions and lay hold on all the people who are in the city and put them in bonds immediately."[33]

The carriers did as they were told. Having lugged the heavy baskets into Joppa, they suddenly unsealed them and the soldiers inside burst forth and captured the city. Eminently satisfied, General Djehuty sent word to the pharaoh that the task of conquering Joppa had been completed with no loss of Egyptian lives.

Modern experts believe that the story of Djehuty's taking of Joppa is a myth because of the way he did it—by a clever trick. Archaeological evidence has revealed that New Kingdom Egyptian military leaders did not work that way. Instead they employed the standard siege tactics of the Middle East in that era, as clearly depicted in a number of elaborate reliefs (carvings raised slightly from a flat surface, usually stone). These tactics included the use of battleaxes to chop through the wooden gates of towns and fortresses; scaling ladders, which attackers placed against the defensive walls and climbed up and over them; archers who fired arrows at the battlements to provide cover for the climbers; and saps, tunnels dug under the walls, either to make them collapse or to gain access to the city or citadel.

That the story is a myth is also seen in the fact that the pharaohs of the New Kingdom, including Tuthmosis, loudly trumpeted their military victories in written accounts and paintings and carved reliefs on palace walls, so had one of Tuthmosis's generals managed to capture an enemy city without losing a single soldier, the king would have used every means at his disposal to brag about it to his people and the world at large. Yet no mention of Djehuty, or anyone

New Kingdom pharaoh Tuthmosis III, depicted in this statue, was helped in his conquest of Palestine and Syria by the noted general Djehuty, who later took on mythic proportions in Egyptian society.

else, taking Joppa by stealth appears in any of Tuthmosis's war records. Also, the tale, which clearly has the signs of being a fable, did not begin to appear until almost two centuries after the taking of Joppa.

The Pharaoh's New Wife

Another real New Kingdom pharaoh, Ramesses II (reigned 1279–1213 B.C.), was a major player in a myth that arose long after that king's own time. In this case, priests in the Egyptian

An Entertaining Shipwreck

One kind of mythical tale that the Egyptians particularly enjoyed was the so-called frame story. It was constructed as a story within a story, so that the narrative began with the first story, which framed the second story. One of the finest examples of this literary device in Egyptian literature was "The Shipwrecked Sailor," which had three frames, or a story within a story within a story. The myth begins with the narrative of a trader who is upset because he can no longer ship gold from a foreign land to enrich the pharaoh's treasury. On the docks, he runs into one of his sailors, who asks why he is so glum. To cheer up his boss, the sailor starts telling him the second story, about how years before he had been on a voyage and his ship had broken up in a storm. Everyone aboard was killed except for him, and he washed ashore on a remote island. There, he encountered a giant talking snake. In time, the man and snake became friends, and the creature told him how it had arrived on the island— thereby beginning the story within the sailor's story, which itself lay within the trader's story. In ancient Egypt, where few people could read and there was no radio, TV, movies, or Internet, cleverly plotted tales like this were a major form of entertainment.

city of Alexandria carved the tale—"The Princess and the Demon"—on a stone marker in the 200s B.C. By that time, the New Kingdom was a distant memory, and members of a family of Greek kings, the Ptolemies, ruled the country.

The story told in the myth begins with King Ramesses traveling to Syria, north of Palestine, intending to collect tribute (payment acknowledging submission to a conqueror) from some local rulers. Not wanting to pick a fight with Egypt's mightiest pharaoh in recent memory, one of these rulers, the king of Bakhtan, promptly sent the required tribute. It consisted of several wagons filled with bronze and other metals, valuable jewelry, finely made cloth, and other costly commodities.

In addition to these standard items, the ruler of Bakhtan sent an exceptional gift—his eldest daughter, who was extremely beautiful. It was expected that the young woman would join Ramesses' harem. This reference in the myth reflected the fact that Egyptian pharaohs customarily had multiple wives, who dwelled in a special suite of rooms in a designated section of the royal palace. It should be noted that the role of these wives was not simply to be intimate

In this limestone relief, Ramesses II makes an offering to Amun-Ra and Khonsu to commemorate the gods' help in healing Maat-nefru-Ra's sister.

with the pharaoh. The women were also tasked with raising the king's children and producing most of the clothes worn by members of the royal family. According to Egyptologist Rosalie David, the wives' quarter was the place

> where they carried out their own activities and undertook the early education of their children. [It included] dining halls, bedrooms, and a kitchen. There were also royal residence towns, visited periodically by the king, where queens and other women lived. . . . [Those women] and their female servants produced high-quality textiles, including the royal garments, on a large scale.[34]

At first, Ramesses planned to send the young woman he had been given to one of his royal residence towns. There, older wives would instruct her in the proper rules and courtesies of Egypt's royal court. But this changed as the king got to know her. He was delighted to find that she was keenly intelligent and had a wonderful sense of humor that greatly pleased him. Also, she had numerous talents, among them the ability to read and a sweet, soothing singing voice. Before long, the pharaoh was smitten by the girl, to whom he gave an Egyptian name, Maat-nefru-Ra.

The Ailing Princess

More than a year went by, during which Ramesses was happier than he had ever been. But then word arrived that Maat-nefru-Ra's sister, Bentresh, was gravely ill in faraway Bakhtan. In a letter, that kingdom's ruler told Ramesses that his people lacked skilled doctors and begged the pharaoh to send his best physician to save the princess's life.

Because he loved Maat-nefru-Ra so much, Ramesses was happy to fulfill this request. Wasting no time, he sent his most trusted healer, Djehuty-em-hab, to Bakhtan. When the doctor reached Bentresh's bedside and examined her, he was appalled to find that she had a raging fever caused by a demon that had taken up residence in her body. This would not surprise Egyptians who read or heard this myth. They firmly believed that some ailments were caused by evil de-

The Bentresh stele records the myth of Ramesses and Bentresh's healing.

mons, and a number of doctors were trained in magic spells that would expel those loathsome beings.

In the case of Bentresh's demonic possession, however, the spells employed by Djehuty-em-hab did not work. The detestable creature stubbornly refused to vacate her feverish body. The only way to drive the demon away, the physician told her father, was to ask one of Egypt's gods to come in person and directly assault the monster.

Djehuty-em-hab sent a messenger to inform Ramesses of this dilemma, and the worried pharaoh hurried to the temple of the moon god Khonsu in Thebes. With due reverence, the king called on the deity to go to Bakhtan and heal the stricken princess. The hawk-headed god heard Ramesses' words, took pity on poor Bentresh, and immediately went to her bedchamber. There, he forced the demon out of the girl's body and subdued the nasty spirit.

Khonsu would have slain his adversary, but at the last minute the demon begged the god not to kill it, promising that in exchange for its life it would leave Bakhtan forever. Khonsu agreed to this, and the demon departed. In this way, Bentresh was fully healed, and her father, sister, and Egypt's pharaoh rejoiced and made offerings of thanks to Khonsu.

To Stay or Flee?

While "The Princess and the Demon" reveals certain aspects of Egyptian royal marriage customs, medical beliefs, and magical spells, another popular myth explores the Egyptians' strong belief in divine providence. Over the centuries, they became certain that the gods—at times individually, and always as a whole—believed in fairness and dispensing mercy, sometimes even to sinners. In the average Egyptian's mind, therefore, a spirit of ultimate justice pervaded the universe. It seemed to provide the hope that even if a person's life took some wrong or unexpected turns, there was a chance that things would work out all right in the end.

One of the Egyptians' favorite myths, "The Adventures of Sinuhe," deals with that powerful theme. The story is set in the early Middle Kingdom reign of the pharaoh Senusret I (1965–1920 B.C.), who had succeeded his father, Amenemhat I. The first of many written versions of the myth appeared a bit more than a century later, about 1800 B.C. Some of these texts are so well written, and the story itself is so compelling, that in modern times it has come to be seen as the finest example of ancient Egyptian literature.

Sinuhe was a high-ranking soldier who served in the Egyptian army directly under young Prince Senusret. One night when they were campaigning in Libya, Sinuhe saw some royal messengers slip quietly into the Egyptian camp. Out of curiosity, he followed them to Senusret's tent and secretly listened to what they told the prince.

Was Sinuhe Real?

The myth of Sinuhe's travels involved at least one character who had been a real person—the pharaoh Senusret I. Modern scholars think the title character might also have been real; however, they generally agree that the tale itself is fictional.

More Myths About Ramesses

The famous pharaoh Ramesses II appeared as a major character not only in some Egyptian myths, but also in the lore of the ancient Hebrews, who dwelled in nearby Palestine. For example, the biblical book of Exodus suggests that Ramesses was the "pharaoh of oppression" who had enslaved a large group of Hebrews and forced them to build two new cities for him. The Hebrew prophet Moses went to the pharaoh and demanded that he allow the slaves to leave Egypt. But Ramesses refused. So God brought down ten terrible plagues on Egypt, including swarms of locusts and flies and the death of the firstborn son in every Egyptian family, including the pharaoh's. Overcome with grief, Ramesses agreed to let the slaves go. But soon after they had left, he changed his mind and chased after them. The pharaoh's soldiers were closing in on the escaping Hebrews when God caused the waters of the Red Sea to swallow up the soldiers, drowning them. (It must be noted that archaeologists have found no proof that Ramesses did any of these things nor that the Egyptians ever enslaved large numbers of Hebrews.)

Ramesses II appears in the Bible as the "pharaoh of oppression" who faced Moses's ten plagues before allowing the Hebrews to leave Egypt.

Amenemhat was dead, the messengers said, cut down by assassins' daggers. Senusret was now pharaoh. But some high government officials advised that he keep all this to himself until he returned to Egypt; otherwise, usurpers might take advantage of his absence and seize the throne, causing Egypt to erupt in turmoil.

Hearing these momentous words, Sinuhe grew troubled. Worried that Senusret might discover he knew things he should not, he panicked. "My heart fluttered," Sinuhe said in one of the ancient texts of the myth, which is told in the first person. "My arms spread out, [and] a trembling befell all my limbs. I removed myself in leaps to seek a hiding place."[35]

Sinuhe hid in some bushes until shortly before sunrise and then fled. Avoiding villages and travelers whenever possible, he left Libya and steadily made his way eastward across Egypt to the deserts of the Sinai Peninsula. Then he traveled northward into Palestine, ending up in the land of Retenu (now part of Israel). There, he had the good luck to meet the local king, Ammunenshi, who took a liking to the Egyptian.

Maintaining the Natural Balance

In the years that followed, Sinuhe thrived, later recounting that the kindly Ammunenshi "married me to his eldest daughter" and "made me chief of a tribe in the best part of his land," and "I passed many years, my children becoming strong men, each a master of his tribe."[36]

In return for these favors, the Egyptian fought as an officer in Ammunenshi's army. But finally, Sinuhe became too old to fight and started to long for his native land of Egypt. He humbly begged his father-in-law to allow him to return there to live out his days.

Ammunenshi assented, and Sinuhe journeyed back to Egypt. The former exile worried that Senusret, who was still pharaoh, might not approve of his return or might even punish him. But these things did not happen. In fact, the king graciously welcomed Sinuhe back, and when he learned why Sinuhe had fled years before, Senusret said it was a shame he had felt the need to run. Still, the pharaoh pointed out, the gods worked in mysterious ways. They knew why Sinuhe had fled. In their eyes he was a good man who had made a mistake, and as long as he lived far from the land where he belonged—Egypt—nature was out of balance. So when he returned to his native land, they were pleased to see that balance restored. Thus did Sinuhe spend his final years happily in the beloved country of his birth.

The Egyptians called that balance of the universal order *ma'at,* which was sometimes visually represented by the scales of justice. They believed that when the natural order was out of balance, chaos and injustice could result. So it is not surprising that they found the story of Sinuhe so appealing. Fear had caused him to flee abroad, pushing *ma'at* ever so slightly out of balance. When he finally returned, the natural balance was restored, and all was well with Egypt and the world.

CHAPTER 5

The Egyptian Myths in Pop Culture

gyptian mythology, with its colorful gods, heroes, and multiple creation tales, was always a reflection of the unique, vibrant, and long-lived society that spawned it. Moreover, many of its legendary deities and human characters were so appealing that they outlived the ancient Egyptian nation by a considerable number of centuries. First, other Mediterranean peoples and societies adopted some of those gods, along with their myths. Later, European nations developed the science of archaeology, and through it they rediscovered the splendor of ancient Egypt, including its complex religious beliefs and myths.

For these reasons, several Egyptian myths and characters live on in what historian David Silverman has called "the high visibility of ancient Egypt to the popular imagination."[37] Some people are drawn to these ancient tales and gods because of the exotic look of their settings and costumes in artistic renderings. Others are fascinated by the way so many of the myths delve into the mysteries of death, rebirth, and eternal life.

Whatever may attract members of each new generation to the Egyptian myths, these stories have become permanent fixtures of Western culture, including popular culture. Often called "pop" or "mass" culture for short, it is the sum

of historical events and figures, customs, ideas, attitudes, and visual images shared by most Americans, British, and other Westerners. In particular, these myths have come to pervade the modern art, literature, and entertainment media. "It is an important testimony to the power" of Egyptian mythology, scholar Joshua J. Mark notes, "that so many works of the imagination, from films to books to paintings, have been inspired by it."[38]

The Luxor hotel in Las Vegas, Nevada, was inspired by what has been called "the high visibility of ancient Egypt to the popular imagination."

Egypt in Decline

It should be noted that this spectacular survival of the Egyptian myths was far from inevitable. In fact, looking back at the long historical march of the ancient Mediterranean peoples, for a while the Egyptian nation and its culture were seriously threatened with extinction. The New Kingdom, the period in which the pharaohs had reached outward and created an empire encompassing large sections of the Middle East,

Isis in Roman Eyes

After the worship of Isis became common in the Roman lands, many people came to imagine that goddess as described by the writer Lucius Apuleius in his popular second-century A.D. *novel* The Golden Ass. *In one pivotal scene, Isis enters a dream of the troubled main character, Lucius, and tells him,*

Behold Lucius, I am come. Your weeping and prayers have moved me to help you. I am she that is the natural mother of all things, mistress and governess of all the elements, the initial progeny of worlds, chief of powers divine, Queen of heaven, the principal of the Gods celestial, the light of the goddesses. At my will the planets of the air, the wholesome winds of the Seas, and the silences of hell be obedient. My name, my divinity is adored throughout all the world in diverse manners, in variable customs and in many names. . . . Behold, I am come to take pity on your fortune and tribulation. Behold, I am present to favor and aid you. Stop your weeping and lamentation and put away your sorrow, for behold the healthful day which is ordained by my providence.

Apuleius. *The Golden Ass.* Adapted by Paul Halsall from a 1566 translation. Ancient History Source Book. www.fordham.edu/halsall/ancient/lucius-assa.asp.

The worship of Isis spread throughout the Roman Empire in the first century B.C.

proved to be the last gasp of a strong independent Egypt. That momentous era ended in 1069 B.C. with the death of Ramesses XI, the last of the successors and namesakes of the great pharaoh Ramesses II.

Thereafter, Egypt, already in decline, was wracked by civil strife and disunity. It grew progressively weaker under a series of unimpressive rulers until 674 B.C., when the warlike Assyrians, from Mesopotamia (now Iraq), invaded and seized much of the country. Assyria itself was invaded and destroyed soon afterwards, in 612 B.C. But the next foreign incursion into Egypt came in 525 B.C. with the arrival of the Persians, who had recently overrun most of the Middle East. The Egyptians remained under the Persian yoke until 332 B.C., when the Macedonian-Greek king Alexander III (later called "the Great") liberated it during his own conquest of Persia.

Egypt was hardly free, however. Soon after Alexander's untimely death in 323 B.C., one of his leading followers, Ptolemy (TAW-luh-mee), seized Egypt and launched a Greek

By the time of the last pharaoh, Cleopatra VII, Egypt had become weak and ineffectual and was finally absorbed by Rome.

dynasty (family line of rulers) there. The Ptolemies controlled Egypt until the last of them—Cleopatra VII—was defeated by the Romans in 30 B.C. By that time, the formerly great Egyptians had become so weak and ineffectual as to be a laughingstock in the Mediterranean world. The man who defeated Cleopatra, Octavian (who soon afterward became Augustus, the first Roman emperor), summed up Egypt's abysmal image at that moment in time, saying, "Would we not utterly dishonor ourselves if, after surpassing all other nations in valor, we then meekly endured the insults of this rabble, the natives of Alexandria and of Egypt, for what more ignoble or exact name could one give them?"[39]

Influences on Neighboring Peoples

Having already languished under foreign rule for hundreds of years, for the rest of antiquity (ancient times) Egypt remained a Roman province. Yet while the grand, independent Egyptian nation of yesteryear was gone, major facets of Egyptian culture remained firmly entrenched. In particular, Egypt's singular religion and large collection of myths had long since made a powerful mark on the Greeks, Romans, and numerous other neighboring peoples.

A number of Egyptian gods, for instance, were eagerly adopted by these peoples in the first millennium B.C. The cult (collected beliefs, rituals, and myths) of the goddess Isis was the most prominent example. Her worship and highly appealing myths spread first to Palestine and Syria; then to Asia Minor (now Turkey) and the large nearby islands of Cyprus, Rhodes, and Crete; next into mainland Greece; and finally to Roman Italy and beyond that to the farthest reaches of Rome's empire, including distant Britain.

To the Greeks and Romans, Isis was a compassionate mother figure. Among the major rituals of her worship in the Greco-Roman lands were a formal initiation into the congregation and a baptism. Especially popular was her magical resurrection of Osiris in their primary myth and how that story generated the promise of eternal salvation in the afterlife for people who had led decent, virtuous lives.

Early Christian Imagery

Some of the most extensive influences that Egypt's religious lore and myths had on other Mediterranean peoples and groups were on the early Christians. Their faith had arisen in Palestine in the mid-first century A.D. It entered Egypt later in that century, and in the years that followed it steadily spread across the region. The Egyptians more easily identified with and embraced the concept of Jesus as the son of God than did most other Mediterranean peoples of that era. This was because Egypt had the precedent of a similar concept in its own mythology—the idea that the pharaoh was an incarnation and son of a god.

Egyptian converts to Christianity were expected to discard the religious beliefs and rituals of their ancestors, and for the most part they did. However, they held on to a few, which influenced the way the Christian faith developed thereafter. One holdover consisted of traditional images of the Egyptian gods, which remained vivid in each new generation. Over time, for example, some depictions of the great battle between Seth and Horus, in which the latter was avenging Seth's murder of Osiris, showed Horus as a mounted, armored knight. This warrior used a spear to impale Seth, who was depicted as a large, ugly crocodile. A number of modern experts see this imagery as the basis for some later medieval artistic versions of St. George's famous defeat of a dragon.

Another example of ancient Egyptian mythology's affect on emerging Christian imagery was a vivid vision of hell. Classic Egyptian myths contained graphic descriptions of what happened to souls that failed to pass the judgment of the dead in the afterlife. They included horrendous tortures and suffering, including being eaten by bloodthirsty demons. These images strongly influenced the first Christian depictions of hell.

Even more significant in shaping early Christian imagery were visual depictions of Isis and Horus together. The

Egyptians had long perpetuated artistic renderings of that important mythical mother-figure gently and reverently cradling her infant. These images became the chief model on which the first several generations of Christians based their nearly identical pictures of Mary holding the child Jesus. As Egyptologist Erik Hornung says, "There was an obvious analogy between the Horus child and the baby Jesus and the care they received from their sacred mothers. Long before Christianity, Isis had borne the epithet 'mother of the god.'"[40]

From Religion to Art to Escapism

Indirect transmission through Christian imagery was one way that aspects of Egyptian mythology eventually reached the modern world. More direct and fulsome was the rediscovery of ancient Egyptian culture, including its religion and myths, by the emerging discipline of archaeology in the late 1700s and throughout the 1800s. People in Europe, North America, and in other corners of the globe were fascinated by the major ancient Egyptian myths. In large part, they were attracted to the colorful, at times startling images of the gods and other major characters in paintings, sculptures, jewelry, and other artistic forms. This appeal remains strong today. Art, including objects in museums and photos of them in magazines and coffee-table and children's books, remains the primary channel through which the general public is exposed to the characters of Egyptian myths. Bob Brier explains:

> For an ancient civilization to have an impact on modern culture, it must . . . be accessible. That's where Egyptian art comes in, as a window through which everybody, not just scholars, can see something of life along the Nile thousands of years ago. There are statues of gods and goddesses, reliefs of pharaohs and queens, and tomb paintings with scenes of daily activities. And what do people look for in this inviting ancient landscape? Egyptomania seems to have three focal points: the Egyptian pursuit of immortality, a belief that the Egyptians had secret or profound knowledge, and simple escapism.[41]

For most people today, escapism is synonymous with entertainment. In turn, books (including graphic novels), television, movies, and video games are the chief entertainment venues for modern representations of the gods, monsters, and human heroes of Egyptian myths. These depictions are sometimes accurate. That is, they show a character in the same context and manner in which the ancient Egyptians pictured it. By contrast, other modern versions take considerable dramatic license. Often they place the character in a different context or setting, or give it powers, motivations, or goals it did not have in the original myths.

From Phony Gods to Superheroes

A clear example of such dramatic license is the way the great sun god Ra was portrayed in the big-budget 1994 film *Stargate.* The character retained his traditional vibrant imagery, including stunning costumes, jewelry, amulets, and a finely decorated throne. In this case, however, his image as the sun god is merely a sham or ruse to hide his true identity. In reality, he is an alien being from another solar system who has come to earth to exploit its residents for his own purposes. Although the ancient Egyptians had been fooled by him—interpreting his advanced technology as divine or magical powers—a team of modern soldiers and scientists expose him for what he is and destroy him. Sequels and spin-offs to the film included four TV series (*Stargate SG-1, Stargate Atlantis, Stargate Universe,* and *Stargate Infinity*), novels, video games, and comic books. These regularly depicted the Ra character and several other Egyptian gods and their mythical imagery.

Thoth, the god of scribes, knowledge, and architecture, who offered to help the wounded Horus and Seth in the Myth of Kingship, has also had considerable exposure in modern entertainment venues. Among the many novels in which Thoth plays a direct or indirect role are those in a trilogy by Australian writer Matthew Reilly. In the first book, *Seven Ancient Wonders,* the reader is introduced to the "Word of Thoth." A special language derived from ancient Egyptian hieroglyphics, it is vital to a small group of modern archaeologists and military agents who are trying to harness a fantastic, naturally occurring force. This volume and its two sequels are filled with references to Thoth and his mythical abilities and symbols.

Thoth was also the inspiration for the evil wizard Thoth-Amon in "The Phoenix on the Sword" and other short stories by Robert E. Howard (who died in 1936). The so-called father of the modern sword and sorcery genre, Howard was strongly influenced by ancient Egyptian culture and religion. He combined various aspects of Thoth and other gods to create Thoth-Amon, whom he envisioned as a member of a very ancient race that eventually gave rise to ancient Egyptian civilization. In the 1980s, the creators of the popular, very complex computer game NetHack borrowed Thoth-Amon. In the game, he was one of several mythical characters whose favor players had to gain in order to move from level to level.

A number of other gods and heroes from the ancient Egyptian myths became comic book characters, including superheroes, during the twentieth century. These included both Isis and her mythical brother-husband Osiris. In the vast DC Comics universe, Isis is a modern woman named Andrea Thomas who becomes a superhero by channeling the powers of the ancient Isis and a few other Egyptian deities. Similarly, another DC Comics hero, Hawkman, believes that he has special powers because he is the reincarnation of an ancient Egyptian prince. His modern name symbolizes the common Egyptian religious custom of combining animal and human traits in a single character. Meanwhile, Marvel Comics has its share of Egyptian-inspired superheroes. Among them is

In the film Stargate *an alien dons the trappings of the sun god Ra and comes to earth to exploit its residents for his own purposes.*

Moon Knight, whose powers derive from Khonsu, the moon god who defeated the demon in "The Princess and the Demon." Another Marvel hero, Earth Lord, is a modern man whom the ancient god Seth seeks out and gives an array of special abilities in order to better serve that deity.

Baskets, Jars, and a Wooden Horse

The ancient Egyptians had their own mythical human heroes, of course, many of them based on real people, and some of them have been incorporated into stories, films, and other modern entertainment forms. One example, however, the story of Djehuty and his baskets containing armed fighters, did not have to wait until modern times to inspire other

Odysseus the Greek Djehuty?

Some modern historians think that the episode of the Trojan horse in Greek mythology was based on the Egyptian tale of General Djehuty and his use of trickery to capture the city of Joppa. These scholars point out that the early inhabitants of mainland Greece had conducted long-distance trade with the Egyptians, so at least some Greeks were familiar with common Egyptian myths, of which Djehuty's tale was widely popular. The Greek myth of the Trojan War, including the part about the horse, developed bit by bit between about 1200 and 800 B.C. Homer, the Greek poet who described this war in his epic poem the *Iliad* in the 700s B.C., did not depict the horse in that work. And he mentioned it only very briefly in his other epic, the *Odyssey*. But it appears that earlier Greek poets added the horse episode to the myth, perhaps basing it on the Egyptian story. If they did indeed model the horse-shaped vessel containing hidden soldiers on Djehuty's baskets, then Odysseus, the Greek king credited with conceiving the idea of the Trojan horse, was the Greek version of General Djehuty.

artists. Some scholars think that the Trojan Horse (or Wooden Horse) from the famous Greek myth of the Trojan War may have been based on it.

When the Greeks attacked Troy, on the coast of Asia Minor, the story went, one of their leaders, Odysseus, conceived a plan to sack the city by sneaking soldiers inside. The first known ancient writer to describe that plan in detail was the Roman epic poet Virgil. In his *Aeneid,* he told how the Greeks constructed an enormous, hollow wooden horse and "secretly hid selected troops inside its dark void, till its whole huge cavernous belly was stuffed with men at arms."[42] Then the rest of the army pretended to give up and sail away. The Trojans thought the horse was an offering to the gods, so they dragged it into the city and celebrated the end of the war. That night, when they were all asleep, the soldiers inside the horse crawled out and opened the gates for their army, which had returned under the cover of darkness. Thus, just as General Djehuty's soldiers had slipped into Joppa inside baskets, Greek commandos sneaked into Troy inside a hollow horse.

An almost equally famous later story that employed the same theme was "Ali Baba and the Forty Thieves." Of uncertain date, it is a Middle Eastern tale that at some point found its way into the famous collection of folktales known as the *One Thousand and One Nights* (also called *The Arabian Nights*). One of the highlights of the story is a scene in which several robbers smuggle themselves into a town inside large leather jars. Many scholars think this episode was also based on the Egyptian myth of General Djehuty.

Imhotep and Sinuhe Resurrected

Another real Egyptian who later figured in mythology and remains popular today is Imhotep, builder of Egypt's first pyramid. During its renowned cycle, or series, of classic horror films in the 1930s and 1940s, Universal Studios resurrected him for what was essentially a new myth. The 1932 movie

King Tut's Curse

Modern fascination for mythical Egyptian curses reached its height in the 1920s. Not long after the discovery of the tomb of "King Tut" in 1922, several individuals connected with the excavations died, and some people suggested an ancient curse had killed them.

The Mummy depicted him as an ancient Egyptian named Prince Imhotep, whose mummified corpse was reanimated in the twentieth century. He was played by Boris Karloff (who also played Frankenstein's monster in Universal's first Frankenstein film). To cover up a series of murders he has committed, Imhotep blends into modern society, adopting a secret alias—Ardeth Bay (an anagram of the words "Death by Ra").

The tales of Imhotep have been resurrected many times in movies, the latest being the 2001 film The Mummy Returns.

The mythical Imhotep was also employed in a popular 1985 video game of that name. In the story behind the drama on the screen, Imhotep learned that a beautiful princess possessed books containing the secret of how to make Egypt more fertile. He wanted to obtain those books but had no idea where the princess was. So he sought out the wise god

Thoth (in one of his many modern video game roles), who divulged that she lived on the far side of a vast desert. Imhotep struck out across the desert, but there found himself under attack by warlike nomads who shot white missiles at him. The person playing the game took on Imhotep's persona and shot back at the nomads with the goal of killing them all and reaching the princess.

Still another popular character from ancient Egyptian mythology who is featured in modern entertainment is the famous wanderer Sinuhe. He appeared in several twentieth-century short stories and novels, among which two gained international readership. The first was the story "Awdat Sinuhi," published in 1941 by Nobel Prize–winning Egyptian writer Naguib Mahfouz. Although he kept many aspects of the original myth intact, Mahfouz added a subplot about a lover's triangle to increase the dramatic impact.

The same myth was the partial inspiration for the world-famous, best-selling 1945 novel *The Egyptian,* by Finnish writer Mika Waltari.

This sweeping, at times moving story keeps the plot device of having Sinuhe go into exile in a foreign land. There, also as in the original tale, he gains considerable success and later returns to Egypt.

However, Waltari, who was an ardent history buff, chose to change the time and setting from the Middle Kingdom to the reign of the controversial New Kingdom pharaoh Akhenaten (1352–1336 B.C.). That king launched a religious revolution in which he tried to replace the traditional Egyptian deities with what he believed was the sole god—Aten. In the novel, Sinuhe, a young aspiring doctor, is befriended by Akhenaten. Eventually, the pharaoh's spiritual crusade fails, as it did in real life, but Sinuhe becomes hooked by the concept of monotheism and converts to the doomed faith.

In 1954, Twentieth-Century Fox released a spectacular film version of Waltari's novel, also titled *The Egyptian.* It starred Edmund Purdom as Sinuhe, Victor Mature as his friend (and a future pharaoh) Horemheb, and Michael Wilding as Akhenaten. The movie faithfully reproduces much of the plot of the book. Yet what makes the film version

Mika Waltari's 1945 novel The Egyptian *was turned into a movie in 1954. It is known for its extraordinarily accurate depiction of ancient Egyptian society.*

particularly satisfying (and still well worth seeing) is the extraordinary job its makers did in accurately capturing ancient Egyptian society. "The atmospheric sets," University of Arizona historian Jon Solomon writes,

> bring to life a culture that thrived thirty-three centuries ago. The street scenes on the waterfront of Thebes hum with the sound of stone-cutters and the sights of carpenters using string saws, porters hustling to and fro, and slaves bearing the wealthy on litters. The scenes create a unique window through which the modern viewer can briefly glimpse ancient Egypt.[43]

Of special importance for the modern fascination with Egyptian myths, Solomon continues, are the desolate vistas of the burial plots of the pharaohs in "the Valley of the Kings and the fume-filled embalming factory," where mummies were created. These "remind us that the ancient Egyptians were as obsessed by life after death as they were with life itself."[44]

Aten's Face

The "maverick pharaoh" Akhenaten and his followers believed that the blindingly bright disk of the sun was literally the face of Aten, the sole god they worshipped.

The Undiscovered Country

For an ancient Egyptian, that "life after death" occurred in the kingdom ruled by Osiris, whom magical Isis had resurrected. Moreover, it lay in the mysterious nether realm where almighty Ra journeyed each night. In their relentless quest to understand and prepare themselves for existence in such places, the ancient Egyptians produced some of history's most mystical and mesmerizing myths. That "undiscovered country" from which "no traveler returns,"[45] as seventeenth-century English playwright William Shakespeare described death, still both disquiets and fascinates humanity. As a result, many Egyptian myths are as fresh and enticing today as they were when they emerged more than forty centuries ago at the veritable dawn of civilization.

NOTES

Introduction: Myths That Left the World Richer

1. Quoted in *Times of Israel* Staff and AP. "Anti-Islam Movie Sparks Riots in Egypt; Angry Mob Kills American in Libya." *Times of Israel,* September 12, 2012. www.timesofisrael.com/anti-islam-movie-funded-by-100-jewish-donors-producer-tells-wall-street-journal.
2. Herodotus. *The Histories.* Translated by Aubrey de Sélincourt. New York: Penguin,1972, p. 143.
3. Herodotus. *The Histories,* pp. 129–130, 187.
4. Herodotus. *The Histories,* pp. 150–151.
5. Herodotus. *The Histories,* p. 152.
6. Herodotus. *The Histories,* p. 151.
7. Juvenal. *The Sixteen Satires.* Translated by Peter Green. New York: Penguin, 1999, p. 281.
8. George Hart. *Egyptian Myths.* London: British Museum, 1990, p. 8.

Chapter 1: Origins of Egyptian Gods and Myths

9. Hart. *Egyptian Myths,* p. 7.
10. H.W.F. Saggs. *Babylonians.* Berkeley and Los Angeles: University of California Press, 2000, p. 32.
11. David P. Silverman. "Divinity and Deities in Ancient Egypt." In *Religion in Ancient Egypt,* edited by Byron E. Shafer. Ithaca, NY: Cornell University Press, 1991, pp. 17–18.
12. Leonard H. Lesko. "Ancient Egyptian Cosmogonies and Cosmology." In *Religion in Ancient Egypt,* edited by Byron E. Shafer, pp. 90–91.
13. James P. Allen. "The Celestial Realm." In *Ancient Egypt,* edited by David P. Silverman. New York: Oxford University Press, 1997, p. 115.
14. Herodotus. *The Histories,* p. 144.
15. Quoted in Hany Yousry. "The Complete Pyramid Texts of King Unas." Translated by Raymond O. Falkner et al. http://hanyyousry.wordpress.com/2011/03/14/the-complete-pyramid-texts-of-king-unas-1/.
16. Bob Brier. "Egyptomania: What Accounts for Our Intoxication with Things Egyptian?" *Archaeology,* January–February 2004, p. 18.

Chapter 2: Mythical Accounts of the Creation

17. Vincent A. Tobin. "Creations Myths." In *The Ancient Gods Speak: A Guide to Egyptian Religion,* edited by Donald B. Redford. New York: Oxford University Press, 2002, p. 251.
18. Quoted in Josephine Mayer and Tom Prideaux, eds. *Never to Die: The Egyptians in Their Own Words.* New York: Viking, 1938, p. 25.
19. Quoted in Mayer and Prideaux. *Never to Die,* p. 25.
20. Toby Wilkinson. *The Rise and Fall of Ancient Egypt.* New York: Random House, 2010, p. 17.

21. Wilkinson. *The Rise and Fall of Ancient Egypt,* p. 15.
22. Hart. *Egyptian Myths,* p. 21.
23. Quoted in Lesko. "Ancient Egyptian Cosmogonies and Cosmology," p. 96.

Chapter 3: Osiris, Isis, and the Myth of Kingship

24. Rosalie David. *Handbook to Life in Ancient Egypt.* New York: Oxford University Press, 2007, p. 113.
25. Wilkinson. *The Rise and Fall of Ancient Egypt,* p. 15.
26. Apuleius. *The Golden Ass.* Translated by P.G. Walsh. New York: Oxford University Press, 1995, pp. 219–220.
27. David. *Handbook to Life in Ancient Egypt,* p. 142.
28. Bob Brier. *Ancient Egyptian Magic.* New York: HarperCollins, 2001, p. 169.
29. Quoted in William K. Simpson, ed. *The Literature of Ancient Egypt: An Anthology of Stories, Instructions, and Poetry.* New Haven, CT: Yale University Press, 2003, p. 125.
30. Quoted in Simpson. *The Literature of Ancient Egypt,* p. 125.
31. Ian Shaw, ed. *The Oxford History of Ancient Egypt.* New York: Oxford university Press, 2000, p. 9.

Chapter 4: Myths Based on Real Characters

32. Hart. *Egyptian Myths,* p. 62.
33. Quoted in Yigael Yadin. *The Art of Warfare in Biblical Lands in the Light of Archaeological Study.* Vol. 1. New York: McGraw-Hill, 1963, p. 99.
34. David. *Handbook to Life in Ancient Egypt,* p. 182.
35. Quoted in Miriam Lichtheim. *Ancient Egyptian Literature.* Vol. 1. Berkeley: University of California Press, 1975, p. 224.
36. Quoted in Lichtheim. *Ancient Egyptian Literature,* pp. 226–227.

Chapter 5: The Egyptian Myths in Pop Culture

37. David P. Silverman, ed. *Ancient Egypt.* New York: Oxford University Press, 2003, p. 7.
38. Joshua J. Mark. "Ancient History Encyclopedia: Egypt." September 2, 2009. www.ancient.eu.com/egypt.
39. Quoted in Dio Cassius. *Roman History: The Reign of Augustus.* Translated by Ian Scott-Kilvert. New York: Penguin, 1987, p. 53.
40. Erik Hornung and David Lorton. *The Secret Lore of Egypt: Its Impact on the West.* Ithaca, NY: Cornell University Press, 2002, p. 60.
41. Brier. "Egyptomania," p. 16.
42. Virgil. *The Aeneid.* Translated by Patric Dickinson. New York: New American Library, 2002, p. 29.
43. Jon Solomon. *The Ancient World in the Cinema.* New Haven, CT: Yale University Press, 2001, p. 244.
44. Solomon. *The Ancient World in the Cinema,* p. 245.
45. William Shakespeare. *Hamlet.* Act 3, scene 1, lines 80–81.

antiquity: Ancient times.

archaic: Extremely ancient.

benben: In Egyptian mythology, the primeval mound that was the first dry land to emerge during the Creation.

bimorph: The concept or visual image of a god as part human and part animal.

coarse ware: Inexpensive Egyptian pottery fashioned from Nile River mud.

cosmos: The universe, or all that exists.

Duat: In Egyptian mythology, the little-known region lying beneath the earth; it was thought that the sun god traveled through the *Duat* at night before reemerging into the visible world at dawn.

dynasty: A family line of rulers.

Egyptomania: The modern fascination for ancient Egyptian culture, art, monuments, religion, and myths.

Ennead: The nine gods worshipped and associated with the creation at Heliopolis.

incarnation: The embodiment or physical manifestation of a god or other being or force. In Christian doctrine, for example, Jesus is a human incarnation of God.

inscription: Words or pictures carved into stone or some other surface.

ma'at: The natural and beneficial state of balance within the universe.

mastaba: A flat, bench-like structure in which early Egyptian kings and nobles were entombed.

monad: The original source of the gods.

nesu-bit: One of several names given to an Egyptian pharaoh, it symbolized the ruler's combination of divine and mortal traits.

Ogdoad: The eight gods worshipped and associated with the creation at Hermopolis.

oracle: A message thought to come from the gods, or the sacred site where such a message was given, or the person who delivered the message.

papyrus: A kind of paper the Egyptians made from a water plant.

relief (or bas-relief): A carved image raised partially from a flat surface.

sacrifice: An offering made to honor or appease a god or gods.

shawabti (**or** *shabti*)**:** A figurine representing a menial worker; well-to-do Egyptians placed these in their tombs, believing the worker would toil for the rich person in the afterlife.

tribute: Payment of some sort intended to acknowledge one's submission to someone stronger.

zoomorph: The concept or visual image of a god in animal form.

FOR MORE INFORMATION

Books

Barbara Adams. *Egyptian Mummies.* Buckinghamshire, UK: Shire, 2008. A very informative overview of ancient Egyptian embalming of humans and animals, with a reading level aimed at advanced young readers and up.

Bob Brier. *Ancient Egyptian Magic.* New York: HarperCollins, 2001. An excellent summary of the subject, including clear explanations and examples of spells, amulets, curses, dreams, *shawabtis,* and so on.

Rosalie David. *Handbook to Life in Ancient Egypt.* New York: Oxford University Press, 2007. An excellent general overview of nearly all aspects of ancient Egyptian life.

Rosalie David. *Religion and Magic in Ancient Egypt.* New York: Penguin, 2003. A very informative and readable examination of religion through all periods of ancient Egypt, supported by many primary sources and archaeological finds.

Sheri Doyle. *Understanding Egyptian Myths.* New York: Crabtree, 2012. Discusses how myths about gods and heroes helped the ancient Egyptians understand the world they lived in.

I.E.S. Edwards. *The Pyramids of Egypt.* New York: Penguin, 1993. One of the classic works about the pyramids by one of the leading Egyptologists of the twentieth century.

Zahi Hawass. *Pyramids: Treasures, Mysteries, and New Discoveries in Egypt.* New York: White Star, 2011. Modern Egypt's greatest living archaeologist brings to life the ancient Egyptian pyramids, including the most recent discoveries connected to these famous monuments.

Fiona MacDonald. *Egyptian Myths and Legends.* Chicago: Raintree, 2013. A veteran writer of children's books delivers a simplified overview of the major Egyptian myths for younger readers.

Anthony S. Mercatante. *Who's Who in Egyptian Mythology?* New York: Metro Books, 2002. The review of this volume by *Booklist* reads in part: "This readable dictionary [is] extremely informative as well as entertaining. The entries, arranged in alphabetical order, are an exhaustive collection of everything pertaining to Egyptian mythology."

Donald B. Redford, ed. *The Ancient Gods Speak: A Guide to Egyptian Religion.* New York: Oxford University Press, 2002. The most comprehensive single source of information about Egyptian religion, with nearly a hundred articles by reliable Egyptologists and other scholars.

David P. Silverman, ed. *Ancient Egypt.* New York: Oxford University Press, 2003. A useful general depiction of ancient Egyptian culture, with a large section on religion.

Steven Snape. *Ancient Egyptian Tombs: The Culture of Life and Death.* Hoboken, NJ: Wiley-Blackwell, 2011. An excellent, easy-to-read synopsis of how and where the ancient Egyptians buried their dead.

Lewis Spence. *Ancient Egyptian Myths and Legends.* New York: Barnes and Noble, 2005. This is an updated reprint of noted mythologist Spence's classic book from the 1930s on Egyptian mythology.

John M. White. *Everyday Life in Ancient Egypt.* New York: Dover, 2011. A well-written, accurate examination of ancient Egyptian life.

Richard H. Wilkinson. *The Complete Gods and Goddesses of Ancient Egypt.* London: Thames and Hudson, 2003. A highly comprehensive and useful guide to the Egyptian divinities and the symbols and rituals associated with them.

Richard H. Wilkinson. *The Complete Temples of Ancient Egypt.* London: Thames and Hudson, 2000. Examines all of the known temples from ancient Egypt, some in great detail.

Internet Sources

BBC. "Ancient Egyptian Magic." www.bbc.co.uk/history/ancient/egyptians/magic_01.shtml. A noted expert on ancient Egyptian mythology, Dr. Geraldine Pinch, gives a useful general overview of the subject.

BBC. "The Mummy Maker." www.bbc.co.uk/history/ancient/egyptians/mummy_maker_game.shtml. An interactive game that allows people to take part in the simulated mummification of an Egyptian government official.

Zahi Hawass. "The Discovery of the Tombs of the Pyramid Builders at Giza." www.guardians.net/hawass/buildtomb.htm. Renowned Egyptian archaeologist Hawass describes the recent discovery of a cemetery used by the workers who built the Giza pyramids.

April McDevitt. "The Story of Isis and Osiris." www.egyptianmyths.net/mythisis.htm. A well-written, detailed telling of one of the major ancient Egyptian myths.

PBS: *Nova.* "The Pyramids: The Inside Story." www.pbs.org/wgbh/nova/pyramid. An informative and entertaining resource sponsored by the widely viewed television science series *Nova*, including information on Egyptologist Mark Lehner and his groundbreaking studies and experiments related to ancient Egyptian construction.

Royal Ontario Museum. "Ancient Egypt: Glossary of Egyptian Gods and Goddesses." www.rom.on.ca/programs/activities/egypt/learn/gods.php. Provides a list of the major deities and general information on each.

Royal Ontario Museum. "Ancient Egypt: Temples." www.rom.on.ca/pro

grams/activities/egypt/learn/temples
.php. Tells what these structures
were made from and how they were
used.

Tour Egypt. "Egyptian Mythology."
www.touregypt.net/gods1.htm.
This helpful general introduction to
Egyptian mythology identifies the
major kinds of myths and the leading characters in those stories.

Virtual Egypt.com. "The Shipwrecked
Sailor." www.virtual-egypt.com
/newhtml/texts/myths/sailor.htm.
A comprehensive, entertaining telling of one of the most famous of all
ancient Egyptian legends.

INDEX

PICTURE CREDITS

ABOUT THE AUTHOR

Historian Don Nardo has written numerous acclaimed volumes about ancient civilizations and peoples. Among these are studies of the religious beliefs and myths of those peoples, including the Greeks, Romans, Egyptians, Sumerians, and others. Mr. Nardo also composes and arranges orchestral music. He resides with his wife, Christine, in Massachusetts.

DATE			